Write More Fucking Books!

The 2026 Writer's Planner

Welcome, fellow author. If you've picked up this calendar, chances are you understand something most people don't: writing one book at a time is a luxury you can't afford.

I created this system because I needed it myself. After ghostwriting over 100 books for clients around the world and publishing more than a dozen of my own, I realized something critical.

Traditional planning tools weren't built for writers like us.

They assume one project, one deadline, one finish line. But that's not how we work.

We're in the middle of a dystopian novel while editing a client's memoir. We're drafting a romance on Tuesday and pivoting to a business book on Wednesday. We work across genres, across projects, and sometimes across continents with clients who depend on our ability to deliver consistently and on time.

I searched for a calendar that could handle this reality. One that wouldn't make me feel scattered when I was being strategic. One that acknowledged juggling five books in a month isn't chaos. It's craft. When I couldn't find it, I built it.

This 12 Books in a Year System gives you space to track up to five books per month because your creative life demands it. It's designed for the ghostwriter balancing client deadlines, the multi-genre author building different audiences, and the prolific writer who knows inspiration doesn't wait for one project to finish before sparking the next.

I know what it's like to finish your hundredth book and wonder which one that was. To lose track of progress because you're moving too fast.

To need a bird's-eye view of everything in motion without losing sight of each individual story.

This calendar is your command center. Your creative dashboard. Your proof that what you're doing—writing multiple books, serving multiple audiences, building a sustainable career as an author—isn't just possible. It's exactly what you were meant to do.

Inside, you'll find daily inspiration to fuel your writing sessions. I've included quotes, prompts, and reminders for those days when the words won't come. The social media tracker keeps your author platform growing, because writing a book is only half the battle. Being found is the other half. And the contest tracker ensures you never miss a deadline for awards, submissions, or promotional opportunities that could launch your next book into the spotlight.

Here's to your most organized, productive, and accomplished year yet.

Now let's get to work! *Jody Ortiz*

ISBN- 978-1-962490-14-6

Multi-Project Management System

Write Multiple Books • Stay Organized • Achieve Your Goals

Your Multi-Book Writing System:
- Track up to 5 books in progress simultaneously
- Monthly primary book focus: 3 weeks writing + 1 week editing
- Daily tracking for all active projects
- Social media planning and contest submission tracking
- Monthly projects overview to manage all works in progress

Week 1 - Planning & Initial Writing (Days 1-7):
- Days 1-3: Character development, plot outline, world-building, research
- Days 4-7: Start writing (aim for 25% of manuscript), establish voice, research contests

Week 2 - Intensive Writing (Days 8-14):
- Write middle section (40-50% of manuscript)
- Focus on getting words down without editing
- Build tension and develop relationships
- Draft social media posts, brainstorm cover ideas

Week 3 - Finish First Draft (Days 15-21):
- Complete remaining chapters and climax
- Wrap up all plot threads
- Celebrate finishing the draft!
- Let manuscript rest 1-2 days
- Begin cover design research

Week 4 - Editing & Publishing (Days 22-31):
- Days 1-3: Content editing (plot holes, strengthen scenes, proofread)
- Days 4-5: Cover design, formatting, write blurb and bio
- Days 6-7: Upload to platform, submit to contests, schedule promotions, update website

Finish 1 Book Every Month

12 Books • 12 Months • Unlimited Potential

2026 ANNUAL OVERVIEW
Your Bird's Eye View

JANUARY

Book 1:

_____

Book 2:

_____

Book 3:

_____

Book 4:

_____

Book 5:

_____

FEBRUARY

Book 1:

_____

Book 2:

_____

Book 3:

_____

Book 4:

_____

Book 5:

_____

MARCH

Book 1:

_____

Book 2:

_____

Book 3:

_____

Book 4:

_____

Book 5:

_____

APRIL

Book 1:

_____

Book 2:

_____

Book 3:

_____

Book 4:

_____

Book 5:

_____

MAY

Book 1:

_____

Book 2:

_____

Book 3:

_____

Book 4:

_____

Book 5:

_____

JUNE

Book 1:

_____

Book 2:

_____

Book 3:

_____

Book 4:

_____

Book 5:

_____

JULY

Book 1:

_____

Book 2:

_____

Book 3:

_____

Book 4:

_____

Book 5:

_____

AUGUST

Book 1:

_____

Book 2:

_____

Book 3:

Book 4:

Book 5:

SEPTEMBER

Book 1:

Book 2:

Book 3:

Book 4:

Book 5:

OCTOBER

Book 1:

Book 2:

Book 3:

Book 4:

Book 5:

NOVEMBER

Book 1:

Book 2:

Book 3:

Book 4:

Book 5:

DECEMBER

Book 1:

Book 2:

Book 3:

Book 4:

Book 5:

COLOR CODE YOUR PROJECTS

☐ Client Work

☐ Personal Projects

☐ Fiction

☐ Non-Fiction

☐ Editing/Revision

☐ Research/Planning

2026 GOALS & BIG PICTURE NOTES

_____
_____
_____
_____
_____
_____
_____
_____
_____
_____
_____
_____
_____
_____
_____
_____
_____
_____
_____
_____
_____
_____
_____
_____
_____
_____
_____
_____
_____
_____
_____
_____
_____
_____
_____
_____

Contents

Before you get started….

GHOSTWRITER'S GUIDE TO HIGH-SPEED PRODUCTION
From Someone Who's Written 100+ Books

MINDSET SHIFTS

1. **Kill the myth of "writer's block"** - You're not blocked. You're just afraid the words won't be perfect. Write them anyway. You can't edit a blank page.
2. **Separate writing from editing** - These are different brain modes. Don't edit while drafting. Your inner editor is a productivity killer. Trust me. I struggle with this.
3. **Done is better than perfect** - Clients don't pay for perfection, they pay for completion, and your readers won't know what you didn't write.
4. **Writing is a job, not a mood** - Plumbers don't wait for inspiration. They just do the job. Show up whether you feel like it or not.
5. **Volume creates quality** - You don't get good by writing one perfect sentence. You get good by writing a million imperfect ones.

SPEED TECHNIQUES

6. **Use dictation software** - Talk faster than you type. Dragon NaturallySpeaking or Google Docs voice typing. I sometimes wear a recording device while doing chores. You'll triple your output.
7. **Write out of order** - Stuck on chapter 3? Skip to chapter 7. You don't build a house room by room in order. By the time I write chapter 10 I want to change chapter 3 anyway.
8. **Set a timer, not a word count** - 25 minutes of focused writing (Pomodoro). Time pressure forces output. I've won writing sprints. Try one!
9. **Lower your standards for first drafts** - Aim for 60% good enough. You'll fix it in editing. Perfectionism is procrastination in disguise.

10. **Never end a writing session mid-scene** - Always stop knowing what comes next and write a note so you won't forget. Makes starting tomorrow easier.
11. **Write drunk, edit sober** (metaphorically) - First draft: fast, loose, messy. Second draft: precision and polish.
12. **Use placeholders** - Can't think of a character name? Call them [NAME]. Need to research something? Write [RESEARCH CIVIL WAR DATES] and keep going. Don't get bogged down in the details.

PLANNING THAT ACTUALLY WORKS

13. **Outline in bullet points, not prose** - "Jane discovers secret" not "Jane carefully walks through the dusty basement and discovers..."
14. **Know your ending before you start** - You can't drive to a destination you haven't picked. Wandering wastes time. Where are you heading?
15. **Scene cards, not chapter outlines** - Each scene = one card with goal/conflict/outcome. Rearrange as needed.
16. **Research AFTER drafting** - Write [CHECK THIS] and keep moving. Research is the #1 procrastination tool.
17. **Create character sheets once, reference forever** - Nothing kills momentum like forgetting if your character's eyes are blue or brown.
18. **Use templates for structure** - Romance: meet-cute, obstacle, black moment, resolution. Mystery: body, suspects, red herrings, reveal. Don't reinvent the wheel.

WORKFLOW HACKS

19. **Write at the same time every day** - Train your brain when it's "writing time." Routine eliminates decision fatigue.
20. **Close ALL tabs and apps** - Internet research during writing is a trap. Airplane mode is your friend. I have two Freewrites and I love them. They eliminate distractions completely.
21. **Listen to classical music without words** - Music designed for concentration. Silence is overrated.

22. **Two monitors: outline on one, draft on the other** - No toggling between documents. Saves hours over a book.
23. **Track word count by project, not just daily** - See the actual book growing. Motivating when daily count is low. Figure out your percentage and keep a graph and fill it in.
24. **Batch similar tasks** - Write all dialogue in one pass, then add action beats, then description. When writing multiple points of view, write the story from one perspective and then the other and so on… Assembly line = speed.
25. **Use text expansion software** - Type "mct" and it expands to "Maria Catherine Thompson." Saves thousands of keystrokes per book.

STAMINA BUILDERS

26. **Write in sprints, not marathons** - 25-minute sprints with 5-minute breaks beat 8-hour slogs. Your brain needs rest.
27. **Switch projects when stuck** - Have 3-5 books in rotation. Stuck on one? Jump to another. Momentum matters more than completion order.
28. **Set micro-goals** - "Write 500 words" is easier than "finish chapter 8." Small wins fuel big progress.
29. **Reward yourself immediately** - Finished your sprint? Coffee. Hit 2K words? Walk outside. Brain needs dopamine to keep going and the distraction will fire your creativity.
30. **Track streaks** - Don't break the chain. Even 100 words counts. Momentum is everything.

CLIENT WORK SPECIFICS

31. **Get the full brief upfront** - Revisions kill speed. Pin down tone, length, audience, taboos BEFORE starting.
32. **Set boundaries on revision rounds** - Contract for 2 rounds max. Clients will revise forever if you let them.
33. **Template your processes** - Intake forms, contracts, revision requests. Automate the business side so you can write.
34. **Charge by the project, not the hour** - Fast writers get punished on hourly rates. Project rates reward efficiency and

collect 1/3 of the project budget before writing a word. Set delivery schedule and payment schedule for the remaining amount and overdeliver.

35. **Keep a swipe file** - Good chapter openings, smooth transitions, description phrases. Don't reinvent every time.
36. **Voice match in 5 pages or less** - Read their materials, write a sample, lock in the voice, GO. Don't overthink it.

MENTAL GAME

37. **Your first draft is your vomit draft** - Get it out. It's supposed to be ugly. That's why editing exists.
38. **Count "writing" as writing** - Outlining counts. Character development counts. Scene planning counts. Not just prose.
39. **Perfectionism is fear** - If you're spending 2 hours on one paragraph, you're afraid. Write badly on purpose for 5 minutes. Breaks the spell.
40. **Comparison is poison** - Someone writes slower and makes millions. Someone writes faster and makes nothing. Focus on YOUR numbers.
41. **Celebrate ALL progress** - 200 words is more than zero. Bad writing can be fixed. No writing can't.
42. **You're building a catalog, not a masterpiece** - Each book is practice for the next. I wrote my first book in 9 days. By my 20th book, I knew what I was doing. So will you! Volume beats brilliance for career building.

PHYSICAL SETUP

43. **Ergonomics matter** - Hand pain, back pain, and neck pain kill productivity. Invest in your workspace.
44. **Blue light blocking after 6pm** - Protect your sleep. Exhaustion tanks word count.
45. **Caffeine strategically** - Coffee before writing, not during. You want focus, not jitters.
46. **Move between sprints** - Walk, stretch, pushups. Movement prevents burnout.

47. **Hydrate like an athlete** - Dehydration = brain fog. Keep water at your desk and drink a minimum of 60 ounces per day. Your brain and body need it.

REALITY CHECKS

48. **Some days you'll only hit 500 words** - That's 182,500 words a year. Three novels. You're doing fine.
49. **Fast drafting means MORE editing, not less** - You're trading drafting time for editing time. It's still work, just different.
50. **Not every book needs to be fast** - Personal projects can take longer. Client work needs speed. Know which is which.
51. **Speed is a skill, not a talent** - You get faster by writing more. Your 10th book will be faster than your 1st.
52. **Burnout is real** - If you hit it, stop. Rest. Come back. A week off beats six months of stalled productivity.

THE REAL SECRET

53. There is no secret - You write fast by writing. Every day. Even when it sucks. Especially when it sucks. You show up, you put words down, you move forward. That's it. That's the whole game.

Consistency beats inspiration. Volume beats talent. Done beats perfect.

Now stop reading tips and fill out your planner and go write.

"I get my best ideas when I have nowhere to write them."

— Jody Ortiz

January 2026

Book to complete this month: _____

Genre: _____

Target Word/Page Count: _____

Current Stage: _____

Stage Guide:

- Planning - Outlining, research, character development

- Drafting - Active writing phase

- Revising - Content editing and restructuring

- Editing - Line editing and polishing

- Publishing Prep - Cover design, formatting, contest submissions

- Published - Promotion and marketing phase

Monthly Goals:

- Complete manuscript by day 21
- Finish editing and revisions by day 28
- Design professional cover
- Submit to at least 2 contests or promotional opportunities
- Post on social media 3x per week minimum
- _____
- _____

January 2026 - Projects Overview

Track up to 5 books in progress this month

Book	Title & Genre	Current Stage	Target Words/Pages	Month Goal
PRIMARY				
Book 2				
Book 3				
Book 4				
Book 5				

Book Color Coding Guide: Add highlighters or other shading for quick reference.

Book	Shading/Highlight Reference
PRIMARY (Book 1)	
Book 2	
Book 3	
Book 4	
Book 5	

January writing inspiration at a glance: Add these to your calendar or tape them to your computer or wherever they will inspire you.

January 1	January 2
"You can't use up creativity. The more you use, the more you have." — Maya Angelou	*"There is no greater agony than bearing an untold story inside you."* — Maya Angelou
January 3	**January 4**
"Write what should not be forgotten." — Isabel Allende	*"We write to taste life twice, in the moment and in retrospect."* — Anaïs Nin
January 5	**January 6**
"Words have no power to impress the mind without the exquisite horror of their reality." — Edgar Allan Poe	*"If there's a book that you want to read, but it hasn't been written yet, then you must write it."* — Toni Morrison
January 7	**January 8**
"The role of a writer is not to say what we can all say, but what we are unable to say." — Anaïs Nin	*"You must write every single day of your life. You must lurk in libraries and climb the stacks like ladders to sniff books like perfumes."* — Ray Bradbury

January 9

"Start writing, no matter what. The water does not flow until the faucet is turned on."

— Louis L'Amour

January 10

"The scariest moment is always just before you start."

— Stephen King

January 11

"Don't bend; don't water it down; don't try to make it logical; don't edit your own soul according to the fashion."

— Franz Kafka

January 12

"The first draft is just you telling yourself the story."

— Terry Pratchett

January 13

"I can shake off everything as I write; my sorrows disappear, my courage is reborn."

— Anne Frank

January 14

"We have to continually be jumping off cliffs and developing our wings on the way down."

— Kurt Vonnegut

January 15

"You fail only if you stop writing."

— Ray Bradbury

January 16

"Write hard and clear about what hurts."

— Ernest Hemingway

January 17

"The beautiful part of writing is that you don't have to get it right the first time, unlike, say, a brain surgeon."

— Robert Cormier

January 18

"If you want to be a writer, you must do two things above all others: read a lot and write a lot."

— Stephen King

January 19

"Fill your paper with the breathings of your heart."

— William Wordsworth

January 20

"Writing is its own reward."

— Henry Miller

January 21

"I write to discover what I know."

— Flannery O'Connor

January 22

"The best time for planning a book is while you're doing the dishes."

— Agatha Christie

January 23

"Description begins in the writer's imagination, but should finish in the reader's."

— Stephen King

January 24

"You can always edit a bad page. You can't edit a blank page."

— Jodi Picoult

January 25

"Writing is easy. All you have to do is cross out the wrong words."

— Mark Twain

January 26

"The secret to editing your work is simple: you need to become its reader instead of its writer."

— Zadie Smith

January 27

"Writing a book is a horrible, exhausting struggle, like a long bout of some painful illness."

— George Orwell

January 28

"No tears in the writer, no tears in the reader."

— Robert Frost

January 29

"And by the way, everything in life is writable about if you have the outgoing guts to do it."

— Sylvia Plath

January 30

"Either write something worth reading or do something worth writing."

— Benjamin Franklin

January 31

"Get it down. Take chances. It may be bad, but it's the only way you can do anything really good."

— William Faulkner

January Social Media Planning

Monthly Social Media Goals & Tracking

Platform	Goal Posts	Completed	Content Ideas / Notes
Instagram	_____	_____	
Facebook	_____	_____	
TikTok	_____	_____	
BlueSky	_____	_____	
Threads	_____	_____	
LinkedIn	_____	_____	
YouTube/Shorts	_____	_____	
Pinterest	_____	_____	
Goodreads	_____	_____	
BookBub	_____	_____	
Author Website/Blog	_____	_____	
Other	_____	_____	

Weekly Social Media Content Calendar:

- Week 1: Behind-the-scenes character/plot development
- Week 2: Writing progress updates, word count milestones
- Week 3: First draft completion celebration, cover reveals
- Week 4: Book announcement, pre-order/launch details, contest entries

January Contest & Promotional Opportunities

Track submissions and deadlines

Contest/Opportunity	Deadline	Status	Entry Fee	Notes/Requirements
		☐ Plan ☐ Submit ☐ Done	$_____	
		☐ Plan ☐ Submit ☐ Done	$_____	
		☐ Plan ☐ Submit ☐ Done	$_____	
		☐ Plan ☐ Submit ☐ Done	$_____	
		☐ Plan ☐ Submit ☐ Done	$_____	
		☐ Plan ☐ Submit ☐ Done	$_____	
		☐ Plan ☐ Submit ☐ Done	$_____	
		☐ Plan ☐ Submit ☐ Done	$_____	
		☐ Plan ☐ Submit ☐ Done	$_____	
		☐ Plan ☐ Submit ☐ Done	$_____	

Promotional Opportunities Checklist:

- ☐ Book review blogs and websites
- ☐ BookTok/Bookstagram influencer outreach
- ☐ Goodreads giveaway or promotion

26

- ☐ BookBub featured deal submission
- ☐ Amazon/KDP advertising campaign
- ☐ Author newsletter announcement
- ☐ Podcast interview pitches
- ☐ Local bookstore/library events
- ☐ Cross-promotion with other authors
- ☐ Book club outreach

Week 1 (January 1-7): Writing Week

Primary Book Weekly Task Checklist:

PLANNING & SETUP (Days 1-3):

- ☐ Develop main characters (names, traits, motivations, arcs)
- ☐ Create basic plot outline or beat sheet
- ☐ Define key settings and world-building elements
- ☐ Research any necessary details for authenticity

WRITING BEGINS (Days 4-7):

- ☐ Write opening chapters (aim for 25% of target word count)
- ☐ Daily word count goal: _____ words/day
- ☐ Establish narrative voice and tone
- ☐ Research 2-3 potential contests to enter

Date	Primary Book Progress	Other Books & Tasks	Social Media	Contests & Promos
Thu Jan 1	Words/pages: _____	Book 2: Book 3: Book 4: Book 5:	☐ IG ☐ FB ☐ TikTok ☐ BlueSky ☐ Threads ☐ YT ☐ Blog ☐ Other Prompt: ☐ New Year writing goals & resolutions _____	☐ Research ☐ Prepare entry ☐ Submit _____

Date	Primary Book Progress	Other Books & Tasks	Social Media	Contests & Promos
Fri Jan 2	Words/pages: _____	Book 2: Book 3: Book 4: Book 5:	□ IG □ FB □ TikTok □ BlueSky □ Threads □ YT □ Blog □ Other _____	□ Research □ Prepare entry □ Submit _____
Sat Jan 3	Words/pages: _____	Book 2: Book 3: Book 4: Book 5:	□ IG □ FB □ TikTok □ BlueSky □ Threads □ YT □ Blog □ Other Prompt: □ Workspace/ desk setup reveal _____	□ Research □ Prepare entry □ Submit _____
Sun Jan 4	Words/pages: _____	Book 2: Book 3: Book 4: Book 5:	□ IG □ FB □ TikTok □ BlueSky □ Threads □ YT □ Blog □ Other _____	□ Research 2-3 potential contests to enter □ Prepare entry □ Submit _____

Date	Primary Book Progress	Other Books & Tasks	Social Media	Contests & Promos
Mon Jan 5	Words/pages: _____	Book 2: Book 3: Book 4: Book 5:	☐ IG ☐ FB ☐ TikTok ☐ BlueSky ☐ Threads ☐ YT ☐ Blog ☐ Other _____	☐ Research 2-3 potential contests to enter ☐ Prepare entry ☐ Submit _____
Tue Jan 6	Words/pages: _____	Book 2: Book 3: Book 4: Book 5:	☐ IG ☐ FB ☐ TikTok ☐ BlueSky ☐ Threads ☐ YT ☐ Blog ☐ Other _____	☐ Research 2-3 potential contests to enter ☐ Prepare entry ☐ Submit _____
Wed Jan 7	Words/pages: _____	Book 2: Book 3: Book 4: Book 5:	☐ IG ☐ FB ☐ TikTok ☐ BlueSky ☐ Threads ☐ YT ☐ Blog ☐ Other Prompt: ☐ Reading list for the year _____	☐ Research 2-3 potential contests to enter ☐ Prepare entry ☐ Submit _____

Notes:

_____
_____
_____
_____
_____
_____

Week 2 (January 8-14): Writing Week

Primary Book Weekly Task Checklist:

INTENSIVE WRITING WEEK:

- ☐ Write middle section chapters (aim for 40-50% of total manuscript)
- ☐ Daily word/page count goal: _____ words/pages per day
- ☐ Build tension and develop character relationships
- ☐ Keep notes on continuity issues to fix later
- ☐ Don't edit yet - focus on getting words on the page

MARKETING PREP:

- ☐ Draft social media posts about your writing progress
- ☐ Start thinking about cover concepts

Date	Primary Book Progress	Other Books & Tasks	Social Media	Contests & Promos
Thu Jan 8	Words/pages: _____	Book 2: Book 3: Book 4: Book 5:	☐ IG ☐ FB ☐ TikTok ☐ BlueSky ☐ Threads ☐ YT ☐ Blog ☐ Other _____ ☐ Draft social media posts about your writing progress	☐ Research ☐ Prepare entry ☐ Submit _____

Date	Primary Book Progress	Other Books & Tasks	Social Media	Contests & Promos
Fri Jan 9	Words/pages: _____	Book 2: Book 3: Book 4: Book 5:	☐ IG ☐ FB ☐ TikTok ☐ BlueSky ☐ Threads ☐ YT ☐ Blog ☐ Other _____	☐ Research ☐ Prepare entry ☐ Submit _____
Sat Jan 10	Words/pages: _____	Book 2: Book 3: Book 4: Book 5:	☐ IG ☐ FB ☐ TikTok ☐ BlueSky ☐ Threads ☐ YT ☐ Blog ☐ Other _____	☐ Research ☐ Prepare entry ☐ Submit _____
Sun Jan 11	Words/pages: _____	Book 2: Book 3: Book 4: Book 5:	☐ IG ☐ FB ☐ TikTok ☐ BlueSky ☐ Threads ☐ YT ☐ Blog ☐ Other _____	☐ Research ☐ Prepare entry ☐ Submit _____

Date	Primary Book Progress	Other Books & Tasks	Social Media	Contests & Promos
Mon Jan 12	Words/pages: _____	Book 2: Book 3: Book 4: Book 5:	☐ IG ☐ FB ☐ TikTok ☐ BlueSky ☐ Threads ☐ YT ☐ Blog ☐ Other Prompt: ☐ Writing routine breakdown _____	☐ Research ☐ Prepare entry ☐ Submit _____
Tue Jan 13	Words/pages: _____ s	Book 2: Book 3: Book 4: Book 5:	☐ IG ☐ FB ☐ TikTok ☐ BlueSky ☐ Threads ☐ YT ☐ Blog ☐ Other _____	☐ Research ☐ Prepare entry ☐ Submit _____
Wed Jan 14	Words/pages: _____	Book 2: Book 3: Book 4: Book 5:	☐ IG ☐ FB ☐ TikTok ☐ BlueSky ☐ Threads ☐ YT ☐ Blog ☐ Other _____	☐ Research ☐ Prepare entry ☐ Submit _____

☐ **Keep notes on continuity issues to fix later**

_____

_____

_____

Week 3 (January 15-21): Writing Week

Primary Book Weekly Task Checklist:

FINISH FIRST DRAFT:

- ☐ Complete remaining chapters and conclusion
- ☐ Daily word/page count goal: _____ words/pages per day
- ☐ Write climax and resolution
- ☐ Ensure all plot threads are addressed
- ☐ Celebrate completing first draft!

PREPARATION FOR NEXT WEEK:

- ☐ Let manuscript rest for 1-2 days if possible
- ☐ Begin cover design research and mockups
- ☐ Finalize contest submission list

Date	Primary Book Progress	Other Books & Tasks	Social Media	Contests & Promos
Thu Jan 15	Words/pages: _____	Book 2: Book 3: Book 4: Book 5:	☐ IG ☐ FB ☐ TikTok ☐ BlueSky ☐ Threads ☐ YT ☐ Blog ☐ Other _____	☐ Research ☐ Prepare entry ☐ Submit _____
Fri Jan 16	Words/pages: _____	Book 2: Book 3: Book 4: Book 5:	☐ IG ☐ FB ☐ TikTok ☐ BlueSky ☐ Threads ☐ YT ☐ Blog ☐ Other _____	☐ Research ☐ Prepare entry ☐ Submit _____

Date	Primary Book Progress	Other Books & Tasks	Social Media	Contests & Promos
Sat Jan 17	Words/pages: _____	Book 2: Book 3: Book 4: Book 5:	☐ IG ☐ FB ☐ TikTok ☐ BlueSky ☐ Threads ☐ YT ☐ Blog ☐ Other _____	☐ Research ☐ Prepare entry ☐ Submit _____
Sun Jan 18	Words/pages: _____	Book 2: Book 3: Book 4: Book 5:	☐ IG ☐ FB ☐ TikTok ☐ BlueSky ☐ Threads ☐ YT ☐ Blog ☐ Other _____	☐ Research ☐ Prepare entry ☐ Submit _____
Mon Jan 19	Words/pages: _____	Book 2: Book 3: Book 4: Book 5:	☐ IG ☐ FB ☐ TikTok ☐ BlueSky ☐ Threads ☐ YT ☐ Blog ☐ Other Prompt: ☐ Current WIP teaser _____	☐ Research ☐ Prepare entry ☐ Submit _____

Date	Primary Book Progress	Other Books & Tasks	Social Media	Contests & Promos
Tue Jan 20	Words/pages: _____	Book 2: Book 3: Book 4: Book 5:	☐ IG ☐ FB ☐ TikTok ☐ BlueSky ☐ Threads ☐ YT ☐ Blog ☐ Other _____	☐ Research ☐ Prepare entry ☐ Submit _____
Wed Jan 21	Words/pages: _____ ☐ Celebrate completing first draft!	Book 2: Book 3: Book 4: Book 5:	☐ IG ☐ FB ☐ TikTok ☐ BlueSky ☐ Threads ☐ YT ☐ Blog ☐ Other _____	☐ Research ☐ Prepare entry ☐ Submit _____

Plot thread and/or cover design notes:

_____

_____

_____

_____

_____

_____

_____

_____

_____

_____

Notes:

Week 4 (January 22-31): Editing & Publishing Week

Primary Book Weekly Task Checklist:

EDITING (Days 1-3):

- ☐ Read through entire manuscript, make notes
- ☐ Fix plot holes and continuity errors
- ☐ Strengthen weak scenes and dialogue
- ☐ Cut unnecessary content, tighten prose
- ☐ Proofread for grammar, spelling, typos

COVER & FORMATTING (Days 4-5):

- ☐ Design book cover (Canva, Photoshop, or hire designer)
- ☐ Format manuscript for publication (ebook/print)
- ☐ Write book description/blurb
- ☐ Create author bio if needed

PUBLISHING & PROMOTION (Days 6-10):

- ☐ Upload to publishing platform (KDP, IngramSpark, etc.)
- ☐ Submit to contest(s): _____
- ☐ Submit to contest(s): _____
- ☐ Schedule social media announcement posts
- ☐ Update author website/portfolio
- ☐ Send to beta readers or reviewers

Date	Primary Book Progress	Other Books & Tasks	Social Media	Contests & Promos
Thu Jan 22	Words/pages: _____	Book 2: Book 3: Book 4: Book 5:	☐ IG ☐ FB ☐ TikTok ☐ BlueSky ☐ Threads ☐ YT ☐ Blog ☐ Other Prompt: ☐ Update all platform bios & links _____	☐ Research ☐ Prepare entry ☐ Submit _____
Fri Jan 23	Words/pages: _____	Book 2: Book 3: Book 4: Book 5:	☐ IG ☐ FB ☐ TikTok ☐ BlueSky ☐ Threads ☐ YT ☐ Blog ☐ Other _____	☐ Research ☐ Prepare entry ☐ Submit _____
Sat Jan 24	Words/pages: _____	Book 2: Book 3: Book 4: Book 5:	☐ IG ☐ FB ☐ TikTok ☐ BlueSky ☐ Threads ☐ YT ☐ Blog ☐ Other _____	☐ Research ☐ Prepare entry ☐ Submit _____

Date	Primary Book Progress	Other Books & Tasks	Social Media	Contests & Promos
Sun Jan 25	Words/pages: _____	Book 2: Book 3: Book 4: Book 5:	□ IG □ FB □ TikTok □ BlueSky □ Threads □ YT □ Blog □ Other _____	□ Research □ Prepare entry □ Submit _____
Mon Jan 26	Words/pages: _____	Book 2: Book 3: Book 4: Book 5:	□ IG □ FB □ TikTok □ BlueSky □ Threads □ YT □ Blog □ Other _____	□ Research □ Prepare entry □ Submit _____
Tue Jan 27	Words/pages: _____	Book 2: Book 3: Book 4: Book 5:	□ IG □ FB □ TikTok □ BlueSky □ Threads □ YT □ Blog □ Other _____	□ Research □ Prepare entry □ Submit _____

Date	Primary Book Progress	Other Books & Tasks	Social Media	Contests & Promos
Wed Jan 28	Words/pages: _____	Book 2: Book 3: Book 4: Book 5:	☐ IG ☐ FB ☐ TikTok ☐ BlueSky ☐ Threads ☐ YT ☐ Blog ☐ Other _____	☐ Research ☐ Prepare entry ☐ Submit _____
Thu Jan 29	Words/pages: _____	Book 2: Book 3: Book 4: Book 5:	☐ IG ☐ FB ☐ TikTok ☐ BlueSky ☐ Threads ☐ YT ☐ Blog ☐ Other _____	☐ Research ☐ Prepare entry ☐ Submit _____
Fri Jan 30	Words/pages: _____	Book 2: Book 3: Book 4: Book 5:	☐ IG ☐ FB ☐ TikTok ☐ BlueSky ☐ Threads ☐ YT ☐ Blog ☐ Other _____	☐ Research ☐ Prepare entry ☐ Submit _____
Sat Jan 31	Words/pages: _____	Book 2: Book 3: Book 4: Book 5:	☐ IG ☐ FB ☐ TikTok ☐ BlueSky ☐ Threads ☐ YT ☐ Blog ☐ Other _____	☐ Research ☐ Prepare entry ☐ Submit _____

Notes:

January Review & Reflection

Primary Book Progress:

Status: ☐ Completed ☐ In Progress ☐ On Hold

Words/Pages Written This Month: _____

Progress on Other Books:

Book 2:

_____

Book 3:

_____

Book 4:

_____

Book 5:

_____

What worked well this month:

_____

_____

_____

_____

Challenges and solutions:

_____

_____

_____

_____

February 2026

Book to complete this month: _____

Genre: _____

Target Word/Page Count: _____

Current Stage: _____

Stage Guide:

- Planning - Outlining, research, character development

- Drafting - Active writing phase

- Revising - Content editing and restructuring

- Editing - Line editing and polishing

- Publishing Prep - Cover design, formatting, contest submissions

- Published - Promotion and marketing phase

Monthly Goals:

- Complete manuscript by day 21
- Finish editing and revisions by day 28
- Design professional cover
- Submit to at least 2 contests or promotional opportunities
- Post on social media 3x per week minimum
- _____
- _____

February 2026 - Projects Overview

Track up to 5 books in progress this month

Book	Title & Genre	Current Stage	Target Words/Pages	Month Goal
PRIMARY				
Book 2				
Book 3				
Book 4				
Book 5				

Book Color Coding Guide: Add highlighters or other shading for quick reference.

Book	Shading/Highlight Reference
PRIMARY (Book 1)	
Book 2	
Book 3	
Book 4	
Book 5	

February writing inspiration at a glance: Add these to your calendar or tape them to your computer or wherever they will inspire you.

February 1	February 2
"The role of the writer is to say the unsayable, speak the unspeakable and ask difficult questions." — Salman Rushdie	*"Don't tell me the moon is shining; show me the glint of light on broken glass."* — Anton Chekhov
February 3	**February 4**
"Your intuition knows what to write, so get out of the way." — Ray Bradbury	*"I write because I don't know what I think until I read what I say."* — Flannery O'Connor
February 5	**February 6**
"There is no real ending. It's just the place where you stop the story." — Frank Herbert	*"The difference between the right word and the almost right word is the difference between lightning and a lightning bug."* — Mark Twain
February 7	**February 8**
"You don't start out writing good stuff. You start out writing crap and thinking it's good stuff, and then gradually you get better at it." — Octavia Butler	*"Writing is a socially acceptable form of schizophrenia."* — E.L. Doctorow

February 9

"The most valuable of all talents is that of never using two words when one will do."

—Thomas Jefferson

February 10

"We are cups, constantly and quietly being filled. The trick is knowing how to tip ourselves over and let the beautiful stuff out."

— Ray Bradbury

February 11

"Every secret of a writer's soul, every experience of their life, every quality of their mind is written large in their works."

— Virginia Woolf

February 12

"I kept always two books in my pocket, one to read, one to write in."

— Robert Louis Stevenson

February 13

"Writing is a struggle against silence."

— Carlos Fuentes

February 14

"Words can be like X-rays if you use them properly—they'll go through anything."

— Aldous Huxley

February 15

"Lock up your libraries if you like; but there is no gate, no lock, no bolt that you can set upon the freedom of my mind."

— Virginia Woolf

February 16

"I write to give myself strength. I write to be the characters that I am not. I write to explore all the things I'm afraid of."

— Joss Whedon

February 17

"Writing is like driving at night in the fog. You can only see as far as your headlights, but you can make the whole trip that way."

— E.L. Doctorow

February 18

"Close the door. Write with no one looking over your shoulder. Don't try to figure out what other people want to hear from you; figure out what you have to say."

— Barbara Kingsolver

February 19

"I believe myself that a good writer doesn't really need to be told anything except to keep at it."

— Chinua Achebe

February 20

"You never have to change anything you got up in the middle of the night to write."

— Saul Bellow

February 21

"Stories are a communal currency of humanity."

— Tahir Shah

February 22

"What really knocks me out is a book that, when you're all done reading it, you wish the author that wrote it was a terrific friend of yours."

— J.D. Salinger

February 23

"Write to please just one person. If you open a window and make love to the world, so to speak, your story will get pneumonia."

— Kurt Vonnegut

February 24

"Writing, to me, is simply thinking through my fingers."

— Isaac Asimov

February 25

"We write to discover what we think. We write to find out who we are."

— Julia Cameron

February 26

"If you don't have time to read, you don't have the time or the tools to write. Simple as that."

— Stephen King

February 27

"A word after a word after a word is power."

— Margaret Atwood

February 28

"It's none of their business that you have to learn to write. Let them think you were born that way."

— Ernest Hemingway

February Social Media Planning

Monthly Social Media Goals & Tracking

Platform	Goal Posts	Completed	Content Ideas / Notes
Instagram	_____	_____	
Facebook	_____	_____	
TikTok	_____	_____	
BlueSky	_____	_____	
Threads	_____	_____	
LinkedIn	_____	_____	
YouTube/Shorts	_____	_____	
Pinterest	_____	_____	
Goodreads	_____	_____	
BookBub	_____	_____	
Author Website/Blog	_____	_____	

Weekly Social Media Content Calendar:

- Week 1: Behind-the-scenes character/plot development
- Week 2: Writing progress updates, word count milestones
- Week 3: First draft completion celebration, cover reveals

- Week 4: Book announcement, pre-order/launch details, contest entries

February Contest & Promotional Opportunities

Track submissions and deadlines

Contest/Opportunity	Deadline	Status	Entry Fee	Notes/Requirements
		☐ Plan ☐ Submit ☐ Done	$_____	
		☐ Plan ☐ Submit ☐ Done	$_____	
		☐ Plan ☐ Submit ☐ Done	$_____	
		☐ Plan ☐ Submit ☐ Done	$_____	
		☐ Plan ☐ Submit ☐ Done	$_____	
		☐ Plan ☐ Submit ☐ Done	$_____	
		☐ Plan ☐ Submit ☐ Done	$_____	
		☐ Plan ☐ Submit ☐ Done	$_____	
		☐ Plan ☐ Submit ☐ Done	$_____	

Promotional Opportunities Checklist:

- ☐ Book review blogs and websites
- ☐ BookTok/Bookstagram influencer outreach
- ☐ Goodreads giveaway or promotion
- ☐ BookBub featured deal submission
- ☐ Amazon/KDP advertising campaign
- ☐ Author newsletter announcement
- ☐ Podcast interview pitches
- ☐ Local bookstore/library events
- ☐ Cross-promotion with other authors
- ☐ Book club outreach

Week 1 (February 1-7): Writing Week

Primary Book Weekly Task Checklist:

PLANNING & SETUP (Days 1-3):

- ☐ Develop main characters (names, traits, motivations, arcs)
- ☐ Create basic plot outline or beat sheet
- ☐ Define key settings and world-building elements
- ☐ Research any necessary details for authenticity

WRITING BEGINS (Days 4-7):

- ☐ Write opening chapters (aim for 25% of target word count)
- ☐ Daily word/page count goal: _____ words/pages per day
- ☐ Establish narrative voice and tone
- ☐ Research 2-3 potential contests to enter

Date	Primary Book Progress	Other Books & Tasks	Social Media	Contests & Promos
Sun Feb 1	Words/pages: _____	Book 2: Book 3: Book 4: Book 5:	☐ IG ☐ FB ☐ TikTok ☐ BlueSky ☐ Threads ☐ YT ☐ Blog ☐ Other Prompt: ☐ Favorite character I've created	☐ Research ☐ Prepare entry ☐ Submit _____

Date	Primary Book Progress	Other Books & Tasks	Social Media	Contests & Promos
Mon Feb 2	Words/pages: _____	Book 2: Book 3: Book 4: Book 5:	☐ IG ☐ FB ☐ TikTok ☐ BlueSky ☐ Threads ☐ YT ☐ Blog ☐ Other _____	☐ Research ☐ Prepare entry ☐ Submit _____
Tue Feb 3	Words/pages: _____	Book 2: Book 3: Book 4: Book 5:	☐ IG ☐ FB ☐ TikTok ☐ BlueSky ☐ Threads ☐ YT ☐ Blog ☐ Other _____	☐ Research ☐ Prepare entry ☐ Submit _____
Wed Feb 4	Words/pages: _____	Book 2: Book 3: Book 4: Book 5:	☐ IG ☐ FB ☐ TikTok ☐ BlueSky ☐ Threads ☐ YT ☐ Blog ☐ Other _____	☐ Research ☐ Prepare entry ☐ Submit _____
Thu Feb 5	Words/pages: _____	Book 2: Book 3: Book 4: Book 5:	☐ IG ☐ FB ☐ TikTok ☐ BlueSky ☐ Threads ☐ YT ☐ Blog ☐ Other _____	☐ Research ☐ Prepare entry ☐ Submit _____

Date	Primary Book Progress	Other Books & Tasks	Social Media	Contests & Promos
Fri Feb 6	Words/pages: _____	Book 2: Book 3: Book 4: Book 5:	☐ IG ☐ FB ☐ TikTok ☐ BlueSky ☐ Threads ☐ YT ☐ Blog ☐ Other _____	☐ Research ☐ Prepare entry ☐ Submit _____
Sat Feb 7	Words/pages: _____	Book 2: Book 3: Book 4: Book 5:	☐ IG ☐ FB ☐ TikTok ☐ BlueSky ☐ Threads ☐ YT ☐ Blog ☐ Other _____	☐ Research ☐ Prepare entry ☐ Submit _____

Notes:

_____
_____
_____
_____
_____
_____
_____
_____
_____
_____
_____
_____
_____
_____
_____
_____
_____

Week 2 (February 8-14): Writing Week

Primary Book Weekly Task Checklist:

INTENSIVE WRITING WEEK:

- ☐ Write middle section chapters (aim for 40-50% of total manuscript)
- ☐ Daily word/page count goal: _____ words/pages per day
- ☐ Build tension and develop character relationships
- ☐ Keep notes on continuity issues to fix later
- ☐ Don't edit yet - focus on getting words on the page

MARKETING PREP:

- ☐ Draft social media posts about your writing progress
- ☐ Start thinking about cover concepts

Date	Primary Book Progress	Other Books & Tasks	Social Media	Contests & Promos
Sun Feb 8	Words/pages: _____	Book 2: Book 3: Book 4: Book 5:	☐ IG ☐ FB ☐ TikTok ☐ BlueSky ☐ Threads ☐ YT ☐ Blog ☐ Other _____ ☐ Draft social media posts about your writing progress	☐ Research ☐ Prepare entry ☐ Submit _____

Date	Primary Book Progress	Other Books & Tasks	Social Media	Contests & Promos
Mon Feb 9	Words/pages: _____	Book 2: Book 3: Book 4: Book 5:	☐ IG ☐ FB ☐ TikTok ☐ BlueSky ☐ Threads ☐ YT ☐ Blog ☐ Other _____	☐ Research ☐ Prepare entry ☐ Submit _____
Tue Feb 10	Words/pages: _____	Book 2: Book 3: Book 4: Book 5:	☐ IG ☐ FB ☐ TikTok ☐ BlueSky ☐ Threads ☐ YT ☐ Blog ☐ Other Prompt: ☐ Author crushes/ writing inspirations _____	☐ Research ☐ Prepare entry ☐ Submit _____
Wed Feb 11	Words/pages: _____	Book 2: Book 3: Book 4: Book 5:	☐ IG ☐ FB ☐ TikTok ☐ BlueSky ☐ Threads ☐ YT ☐ Blog ☐ Other _____	☐ Research ☐ Prepare entry ☐ Submit _____

Date	Primary Book Progress	Other Books & Tasks	Social Media	Contests & Promos
Thu Feb 12	Words/pages: _____	Book 2: Book 3: Book 4: Book 5:	☐ IG ☐ FB ☐ TikTok ☐ BlueSky ☐ Threads ☐ YT ☐ Blog ☐ Other _____	☐ Research ☐ Prepare entry ☐ Submit _____
Fri Feb 13	Words/pages: _____	Book 2: Book 3: Book 4: Book 5:	☐ IG ☐ FB ☐ TikTok ☐ BlueSky ☐ Threads ☐ YT ☐ Blog ☐ Other _____	☐ Research ☐ Prepare entry ☐ Submit _____
Sat Feb 14	Words/pages: _____	Book 2: Book 3: Book 4: Book 5:	☐ IG ☐ FB ☐ TikTok ☐ BlueSky ☐ Threads ☐ YT ☐ Blog ☐ Other Prompt: ☐ Love story from your books _____	☐ Research ☐ Prepare entry ☐ Submit _____

☐ **Keep notes on continuity issues to fix later**

_____
_____
_____
_____

Week 3 (February 15-21): Writing Week

Primary Book Weekly Task Checklist:

FINISH FIRST DRAFT:

- ☐ Complete remaining chapters and conclusion
- ☐ Daily word/page count goal: _____ words/pages per day
- ☐ Write climax and resolution
- ☐ Ensure all plot threads are addressed
- ☐ Celebrate completing first draft!

PREPARATION FOR NEXT WEEK:

- ☐ Let manuscript rest for 1-2 days if possible
- ☐ Begin cover design research and mockups
- ☐ Finalize contest submission list

Date	Primary Book Progress	Other Books & Tasks	Social Media	Contests & Promos
Sun Feb 15	Words/pages: _____	Book 2: Book 3: Book 4: Book 5:	☐ IG ☐ FB ☐ TikTok ☐ BlueSky ☐ Threads ☐ YT ☐ Blog ☐ Other _____	☐ Research ☐ Prepare entry ☐ Submit _____
Mon Feb 16	Words/pages: _____	Book 2: Book 3: Book 4: Book 5:	☐ IG ☐ FB ☐ TikTok ☐ BlueSky ☐ Threads ☐ YT ☐ Blog ☐ Other _____	☐ Research ☐ Prepare entry ☐ Submit _____

Designed by Jody Ortiz

Date	Primary Book Progress	Other Books & Tasks	Social Media	Contests & Promos
Tue Feb 17	Words/pages: _____	Book 2: Book 3: Book 4: Book 5:	☐ IG ☐ FB ☐ TikTok ☐ BlueSky ☐ Threads ☐ YT ☐ Blog ☐ Other _____	☐ Research ☐ Prepare entry ☐ Submit _____
Wed Feb 18	Words/pages: _____	Book 2: Book 3: Book 4: Book 5:	☐ IG ☐ FB ☐ TikTok ☐ BlueSky ☐ Threads ☐ YT ☐ Blog ☐ Other _____	☐ Research ☐ Prepare entry ☐ Submit _____
Thu Feb 19	Words/pages: _____	Book 2: Book 3: Book 4: Book 5:	☐ IG ☐ FB ☐ TikTok ☐ BlueSky ☐ Threads ☐ YT ☐ Blog ☐ Other _____	☐ Research ☐ Prepare entry ☐ Submit _____
Fri Feb 20	Words/pages: _____	Book 2: Book 3: Book 4: Book 5:	☐ IG ☐ FB ☐ TikTok ☐ BlueSky ☐ Threads ☐ YT ☐ Blog ☐ Other _____	☐ Research ☐ Prepare entry ☐ Submit _____

Date	Primary Book Progress	Other Books & Tasks	Social Media	Contests & Promos
Sat Feb 21	Words/pages: _____ □ Celebrate completing first draft!	Book 2: Book 3: Book 4: Book 5:	□ IG □ FB □ TikTok □ BlueSky □ Threads □ YT □ Blog □ Other Prompt: □ Reader appreciation post _____	□ Research □ Prepare entry □ Submit _____

67

Plot thread and/or cover design notes:

_____
_____
_____
_____
_____
_____
_____
_____
_____
_____
_____
_____

Notes:

_____
_____
_____
_____
_____
_____
_____
_____
_____
_____
_____
_____
_____
_____
_____
_____
_____
_____
_____
_____
_____
_____
_____

Week 4 (February 22-28): Editing & Publishing Week

Primary Book Weekly Task Checklist:

EDITING (Days 1-3):

- ☐ Read through entire manuscript, make notes
- ☐ Fix plot holes and continuity errors
- ☐ Strengthen weak scenes and dialogue
- ☐ Cut unnecessary content, tighten prose
- ☐ Proofread for grammar, spelling, typos

COVER & FORMATTING (Days 4-5):

- ☐ Design book cover (Canva, Photoshop, or hire designer)
- ☐ Format manuscript for publication (ebook/print)
- ☐ Write book description/blurb
- ☐ Create author bio if needed

PUBLISHING & PROMOTION (Days 6-7):

- ☐ Upload to publishing platform (KDP, IngramSpark, etc.)
- ☐ Submit to contest(s): _____
- ☐ Submit to contest(s): _____
- ☐ Schedule social media announcement posts
- ☐ Update author website/portfolio
- ☐ Send to beta readers or reviewers

Date	Primary Book Progress	Other Books & Tasks	Social Media	Contests & Promos
Sun Feb 22	Words/pages: _____	Book 2: Book 3: Book 4: Book 5:	☐ IG ☐ FB ☐ TikTok ☐ BlueSky ☐ Threads ☐ YT ☐ Blog ☐ Other _____	☐ Research ☐ Prepare entry ☐ Submit _____

Date	Primary Book Progress	Other Books & Tasks	Social Media	Contests & Promos
Mon Feb 23	Words/pages: _____	Book 2: Book 3: Book 4: Book 5:	☐ IG ☐ FB ☐ TikTok ☐ BlueSky ☐ Threads ☐ YT ☐ Blog ☐ Other _____	☐ Research ☐ Prepare entry ☐ Submit _____
Tue Feb 24	Words/pages: _____	Book 2: Book 3: Book 4: Book 5:	☐ IG ☐ FB ☐ TikTok ☐ BlueSky ☐ Threads ☐ YT ☐ Blog ☐ Other _____	☐ Research ☐ Prepare entry ☐ Submit _____
Wed Feb 25	Words/pages: _____	Book 2: Book 3: Book 4: Book 5:	☐ IG ☐ FB ☐ TikTok ☐ BlueSky ☐ Threads ☐ YT ☐ Blog ☐ Other Prompt: ☐ Share writing playlist _____	☐ Research ☐ Prepare entry ☐ Submit _____

Date	Primary Book Progress	Other Books & Tasks	Social Media	Contests & Promos
Thu Feb 26	Words/pages: _____	Book 2: Book 3: Book 4: Book 5:	☐ IG ☐ FB ☐ TikTok ☐ BlueSky ☐ Threads ☐ YT ☐ Blog ☐ Other _____	☐ Research ☐ Prepare entry ☐ Submit _____
Fri Feb 27	Words/pages: _____	Book 2: Book 3: Book 4: Book 5:	☐ IG ☐ FB ☐ TikTok ☐ BlueSky ☐ Threads ☐ YT ☐ Blog ☐ Other _____	☐ Research ☐ Prepare entry ☐ Submit _____ ____
Sat Feb 28	Words/pages: _____	Book 2: Book 3: Book 4: Book 5:	☐ IG ☐ FB ☐ TikTok ☐ BlueSky ☐ Threads ☐ YT ☐ Blog ☐ Other _____	☐ Research ☐ Prepare entry ☐ Submit _____

Notes:

February Review & Reflection

Primary Book Progress:

Status: ☐ Completed ☐ In Progress ☐ On Hold

Words/Pages Written This Month: _____

Progress on Other Books:

Book 2:

_____

Book 3:

_____

Book 4:

_____

Book 5:

_____

What worked well this month:

_____

_____

_____

Challenges and solutions:

_____

_____

_____

March 2026

Book to complete this month: _____

Genre: _____

Target Word/Page Count: _____

Current Stage: _____

Stage Guide:

- Planning - Outlining, research, character development

- Drafting - Active writing phase

- Revising - Content editing and restructuring

- Editing - Line editing and polishing

- Publishing Prep - Cover design, formatting, contest submissions

- Published - Promotion and marketing phase

Monthly Goals:

- Complete manuscript by day 21
- Finish editing and revisions by day 28
- Design professional cover
- Submit to at least 2 contests or promotional opportunities
- Post on social media 3x per week minimum
- _____
- _____

March 2026 - Projects Overview

Track up to 5 books in progress this month

Book	Title & Genre	Current Stage	Target Words/Pages	Month Goal
PRIMARY				
Book 2				
Book 3				
Book 4				
Book 5				

Book Color Coding Guide: Add highlighters or other shading for quick reference.

Book	Shading/Highlight Reference
PRIMARY (Book 1)	
Book 2	
Book 3	
Book 4	
Book 5	

March writing inspiration at a glance: Add these to your calendar or tape them to your computer or wherever they will inspire you.

March 1	March 2
"The desire to write grows with writing." — Desiderius Erasmus	*"Write what disturbs you, what you fear, what you have not been willing to speak about."* — Natalie Goldberg
March 3	**March 4**
"I don't wait for moods. You accomplish nothing if you do that. Your mind must know it has got to get down to work." — Pearl S. Buck	*"Almost all good writing begins with terrible first efforts. You need to start somewhere."* — Anne Lamott
March 5	**March 6**
"You must stay drunk on writing so reality cannot destroy you." — Ray Bradbury	*"There is something delicious about writing the first words of a story. You never quite know where they'll take you."* — Beatrix Potter
March 7	**March 8**
"Not a wasted word. This has been a main point to my literary thinking all my life." — Hunter S. Thompson	*"You can't wait for inspiration. You have to go after it with a club."* — Jack London
March 9	**March 10**
"If you write one story, it may be bad; if you write a hundred, you have the odds in your favor." — Edgar Rice Burroughs	*"Words are a lens to focus one's mind."* — Ayn Rand

March 11	**March 12**
"To produce a mighty book, you must choose a mighty theme." — Herman Melville	*"Writing is the only thing that when I do it, I don't feel I should be doing something else."* — Gloria Steinem

March 13	**March 14**
"The purpose of a writer is to keep civilization from destroying itself." — Albert Camus	*"Writing is a way of talking without being interrupted."* — Jules Renard

March 15	**March 16**
"Ideas are like rabbits. You get a couple and learn how to handle them, and pretty soon you have a dozen." — John Steinbeck	*"I hate writing, I love having written."* — Dorothy Parker

March 17	**March 18**
"Being a writer is like having homework every night for the rest of your life." — Lawrence Kasdan	*"The road to hell is paved with adverbs."* — Stephen King

March 19	**March 20**
"I'm writing a first draft and reminding myself that I'm simply shoveling sand into a box so that later I can build castles." — Shannon Hale	*"In the writing process, the more a story cooks, the better."* — Doris Lessing

March 21

"The greatest part of a writer's time is spent in reading, in order to write; a man will turn over half a library to make one book."
— Samuel Johnson

March 22

"Writing is a job, a talent, but it's also the place to go in your head. It is the imaginary friend you drink your tea with in the afternoon."
— Ann Patchett

March 23

"Writers write. Dreamers talk about it."
— Jerry B. Jenkins

March 24

"I can't write without a reader. It's precisely like a kiss—you can't do it alone."
— John Cheever

March 25

"Plot is no more than footprints left in the snow after your characters have run by on their way to incredible destinations."
— Ray Bradbury

March 26

"Read, read, read. Read everything—trash, classics, good and bad, and see how they do it."
— William Faulkner

March 27

"The best stories don't come from 'good vs. bad' but from 'good vs. good.'"
— Leo Tolstoy

March 28

"I write entirely to find out what I'm thinking, what I'm looking at, what I see and what it means."
— Joan Didion

March 29

"To be a writer is to sit down at one's desk in the chill portion of every day, and to write; not waiting for the little jet of the blue flame of genius to start from the breastbone."
— John Hersey

March 30

"Writing is easy: All you do is sit staring at a blank sheet of paper until drops of blood form on your forehead."
— Gene Fowler

March 31

"I would hurl words into this darkness and wait for an echo, and if an echo sounded, no matter how faintly, I would send other words to tell."

— Richard Wright

March Social Media Planning

Monthly Social Media Goals & Tracking

Platform	Goal Posts	Completed	Content Ideas / Notes
Instagram	____	____	
Facebook	____	____	
TikTok	____	____	
BlueSky	____	____	
Threads	____	____	
LinkedIn	____	____	
YouTube/Shorts	____	____	
Pinterest	____	____	
Goodreads	____	____	
BookBub	____	____	
Author Website/Blog	____	____	

Weekly Social Media Content Calendar:

- Week 1: Behind-the-scenes character/plot development
- Week 2: Writing progress updates, word count milestones
- Week 3: First draft completion celebration, cover reveals

- Week 4: Book announcement, pre-order/launch details, contest entries

March Contest & Promotional Opportunities

Track submissions and deadlines

Contest/Opportunity	Deadline	Status	Entry Fee	Notes/Requirements
		☐ Plan ☐ Submit ☐ Done	$_____	
		☐ Plan ☐ Submit ☐ Done	$_____	
		☐ Plan ☐ Submit ☐ Done	$_____	
		☐ Plan ☐ Submit ☐ Done	$_____	
		☐ Plan ☐ Submit ☐ Done	$_____	
		☐ Plan ☐ Submit ☐ Done	$_____	
		☐ Plan ☐ Submit ☐ Done	$_____	
		☐ Plan ☐ Submit ☐ Done	$_____	
		☐ Plan ☐ Submit ☐ Done	$_____	
		☐ Plan ☐ Submit ☐ Done	$_____	

Promotional Opportunities Checklist:

- ☐ Book review blogs and websites
- ☐ BookTok/Bookstagram influencer outreach
- ☐ Goodreads giveaway or promotion
- ☐ BookBub featured deal submission
- ☐ Amazon/KDP advertising campaign
- ☐ Author newsletter announcement
- ☐ Podcast interview pitches
- ☐ Local bookstore/library events
- ☐ Cross-promotion with other authors
- ☐ Book club outreach

Stage Guide:

- Planning - Outlining, research, character development
- Drafting - Active writing phase
- Revising - Content editing and restructuring
- Editing - Line editing and polishing
- Publishing Prep - Cover design, formatting, contest submissions
- Published - Promotion and marketing phase

Week 1 (March 1-7): Writing Week

Primary Book Weekly Task Checklist:

PLANNING & SETUP (Days 1-3):

- ☐ Develop main characters (names, traits, motivations, arcs)
- ☐ Create basic plot outline or beat sheet
- ☐ Define key settings and world-building elements
- ☐ Research any necessary details for authenticity

WRITING BEGINS (Days 4-7):

- ☐ Write opening chapters (aim for 25% of target word count)
- ☐ Daily word/page count goal: _____ words/pages per day
- ☐ Establish narrative voice and tone
- ☐ Research 2-3 potential contests to enter

Date	Primary Book Progress	Other Books & Tasks	Social Media	Contests & Promos
Sun Mar 1	Words/pages: _____	Book 2: Book 3: Book 4: Book 5:	☐ IG ☐ FB ☐ TikTok ☐ BlueSky ☐ Threads ☐ YT ☐ Blog ☐ Other Prompt: ☐ Writing process deep dive _____	☐ Research ☐ Prepare entry ☐ Submit _____

84

Date	Primary Book Progress	Other Books & Tasks	Social Media	Contests & Promos
Mon Mar 2	Words/pages: _____	Book 2: Book 3: Book 4: Book 5:	☐ IG ☐ FB ☐ TikTok ☐ BlueSky ☐ Threads ☐ YT ☐ Blog ☐ Other _____	☐ Research ☐ Prepare entry ☐ Submit _____
Tue Mar 3	Words/pages: _____	Book 2: Book 3: Book 4: Book 5:	☐ IG ☐ FB ☐ TikTok ☐ BlueSky ☐ Threads ☐ YT ☐ Blog ☐ Other _____	☐ Research ☐ Prepare entry ☐ Submit _____
Wed Mar 4	Words/pages: _____	Book 2: Book 3: Book 4: Book 5:	☐ IG ☐ FB ☐ TikTok ☐ BlueSky ☐ Threads ☐ YT ☐ Blog ☐ Other _____	☐ Research ☐ Prepare entry ☐ Submit _____

Date	Primary Book Progress	Other Books & Tasks	Social Media	Contests & Promos
Thu Mar 5	Words/pages: _____	Book 2: Book 3: Book 4: Book 5:	☐ IG ☐ FB ☐ TikTok ☐ BlueSky ☐ Threads ☐ YT ☐ Blog ☐ Other _____	☐ Research ☐ Prepare entry ☐ Submit _____
Fri Mar 6	Words/pages: _____	Book 2: Book 3: Book 4: Book 5:	☐ IG ☐ FB ☐ TikTok ☐ BlueSky ☐ Threads ☐ YT ☐ Blog ☐ Other _____	☐ Research ☐ Prepare entry ☐ Submit _____
Sat Mar 7	Words/pages: _____	Book 2: Book 3: Book 4: Book 5:	☐ IG ☐ FB ☐ TikTok ☐ BlueSky ☐ Threads ☐ YT ☐ Blog ☐ Other Prompt: ☐ Spring cleaning: organize writing files _____	☐ Research ☐ Prepare entry ☐ Submit _____

Notes:

_____
_____
_____
_____
_____
_____
_____
_____
_____
_____
_____
_____
_____
_____
_____
_____
_____
_____
_____
_____
_____
_____
_____
_____
_____
_____
_____
_____
_____
_____
_____
_____

Week 2 (March 8-14): Writing Week

Primary Book Weekly Task Checklist:

INTENSIVE WRITING WEEK:

- ☐ Write middle section chapters (aim for 40-50% of total manuscript)
- ☐ Daily word/page count goal: _____ words/pages per day
- ☐ Build tension and develop character relationships
- ☐ Keep notes on continuity issues to fix later
- ☐ Don't edit yet - focus on getting words on the page

MARKETING PREP:

- ☐ Draft social media posts about your writing progress
- ☐ Start thinking about cover concepts

Date	Primary Book Progress	Other Books & Tasks	Social Media	Contests & Promos
Sun Mar 8	Words/pages: _____	Book 2: Book 3: Book 4: Book 5:	☐ IG ☐ FB ☐ TikTok ☐ BlueSky ☐ Threads ☐ YT ☐ Blog ☐ Other _____	☐ Research ☐ Prepare entry ☐ Submit _____

Date	Primary Book Progress	Other Books & Tasks	Social Media	Contests & Promos
Mon Mar 9	Words/pages: _____	Book 2: Book 3: Book 4: Book 5:	☐ IG ☐ FB ☐ TikTok ☐ BlueSky ☐ Threads ☐ YT ☐ Blog ☐ Other _____	☐ Research ☐ Prepare entry ☐ Submit _____
Tue Mar 10	Words/pages: _____	Book 2: Book 3: Book 4: Book 5:	☐ IG ☐ FB ☐ TikTok ☐ BlueSky ☐ Threads ☐ YT ☐ Blog ☐ Other _____	☐ Research ☐ Prepare entry ☐ Submit _____
Wed Mar 11	Words/pages: _____	Book 2: Book 3: Book 4: Book 5:	☐ IG ☐ FB ☐ TikTok ☐ BlueSky ☐ Threads ☐ YT ☐ Blog ☐ Other Prompt: ☐ Research methods you use _____	☐ Research ☐ Prepare entry ☐ Submit _____

Date	Primary Book Progress	Other Books & Tasks	Social Media	Contests & Promos
Thu Mar 12	Words/pages: _____	Book 2: Book 3: Book 4: Book 5:	☐ IG ☐ FB ☐ TikTok ☐ BlueSky ☐ Threads ☐ YT ☐ Blog ☐ Other _____	☐ Research ☐ Prepare entry ☐ Submit _____
Fri Mar 13	Words/pages: _____	Book 2: Book 3: Book 4: Book 5:	☐ IG ☐ FB ☐ TikTok ☐ BlueSky ☐ Threads ☐ YT ☐ Blog ☐ Other Prompt: ☐ Celebrate Women's History Month authors _____	☐ Research ☐ Prepare entry ☐ Submit _____
Sat Mar 14	Words/pages: _____	Book 2: Book 3: Book 4: Book 5:	☐ IG ☐ FB ☐ TikTok ☐ BlueSky ☐ Threads ☐ YT ☐ Blog ☐ Other _____	☐ Research ☐ Prepare entry ☐ Submit _____

☐ Keep notes on continuity issues to fix later

_____

_____

_____

_____

_____

_____

_____

_____

_____

_____

_____

_____

_____

_____

_____

_____

_____

Week 3 (March 15-21): Writing Week

Primary Book Weekly Task Checklist:

FINISH FIRST DRAFT:

- ☐ Complete remaining chapters and conclusion
- ☐ Daily word/page count goal: _____ words/pages per day
- ☐ Write climax and resolution
- ☐ Ensure all plot threads are addressed
- ☐ Celebrate completing first draft!

PREPARATION FOR NEXT WEEK:

- ☐ Let manuscript rest for 1-2 days if possible
- ☐ Begin cover design research and mockups
- ☐ Finalize contest submission list

Date	Primary Book Progress	Other Books & Tasks	Social Media	Contests & Promos
Sun Mar 15	Words/pages: _____	Book 2: Book 3: Book 4: Book 5:	☐ IG ☐ FB ☐ TikTok ☐ BlueSky ☐ Threads ☐ YT ☐ Blog ☐ Other _____	☐ Research ☐ Prepare entry ☐ Submit _____

Date	Primary Book Progress	Other Books & Tasks	Social Media	Contests & Promos
Mon Mar 16	Words/pages: _____	Book 2: Book 3: Book 4: Book 5:	☐ IG ☐ FB ☐ TikTok ☐ BlueSky ☐ Threads ☐ YT ☐ Blog ☐ Other _____	☐ Research ☐ Prepare entry ☐ Submit _____
Tue Mar 17	Words/pages: _____	Book 2: Book 3: Book 4: Book 5:	☐ IG ☐ FB ☐ TikTok ☐ BlueSky ☐ Threads ☐ YT ☐ Blog ☐ Other Prompt: ☐ Research methods you use	☐ Research ☐ Prepare entry ☐ Submit _____
Wed Mar 18	Words/pages: _____	Book 2: Book 3: Book 4: Book 5:	☐ IG ☐ FB ☐ TikTok ☐ BlueSky ☐ Threads ☐ YT ☐ Blog ☐ Other _____	☐ Research ☐ Prepare entry ☐ Submit _____

Date	Primary Book Progress	Other Books & Tasks	Social Media	Contests & Promos
Thu Mar 19	Words/pages: _____	Book 2: Book 3: Book 4: Book 5:	☐ IG ☐ FB ☐ TikTok ☐ BlueSky ☐ Threads ☐ YT ☐ Blog ☐ Other _____	☐ Research ☐ Prepare entry ☐ Submit _____
Fri Mar 20	Words/pages: _____	Book 2: Book 3: Book 4: Book 5:	☐ IG ☐ FB ☐ TikTok ☐ BlueSky ☐ Threads ☐ YT ☐ Blog ☐ Other _____	☐ Research ☐ Prepare entry ☐ Submit _____
Sat Mar 21	Words/pages: _____	Book 2: Book 3: Book 4: Book 5:	☐ IG ☐ FB ☐ TikTok ☐ BlueSky ☐ Threads ☐ YT ☐ Blog ☐ Other Prompt: ☐ Productivity tips & hacks _____	☐ Research ☐ Prepare entry ☐ Submit _____

Plot thread and/or cover design notes:

_____
_____
_____
_____
_____
_____
_____
_____
_____
_____
_____
_____
_____

Notes:

_____
_____
_____
_____
_____
_____
_____
_____
_____
_____
_____
_____
_____
_____
_____
_____
_____
_____
_____
_____
_____
_____
_____
_____
_____

Week 4 (March 22-31): Editing & Publishing Week

Primary Book Weekly Task Checklist:

EDITING (Days 1-3):

- ☐ Read through entire manuscript, make notes
- ☐ Fix plot holes and continuity errors
- ☐ Strengthen weak scenes and dialogue
- ☐ Cut unnecessary content, tighten prose
- ☐ Proofread for grammar, spelling, typos

COVER & FORMATTING (Days 4-5):

- ☐ Design book cover (Canva, Photoshop, or hire designer)
- ☐ Format manuscript for publication (ebook/print)
- ☐ Write book description/blurb
- ☐ Create author bio if needed

PUBLISHING & PROMOTION (Days 6-10):

- ☐ Upload to publishing platform (KDP, IngramSpark, etc.)
- ☐ Submit to contest(s): _____
- ☐ Submit to contest(s): _____
- ☐ Schedule social media announcement posts
- ☐ Update author website/portfolio
- ☐ Send to beta readers or reviewers

Date	Primary Book Progress	Other Books & Tasks	Social Media	Contests & Promos
Sun Mar 22	Words/pages: _____	▪ Book 2: ▪ Book 3: ▪ Book 4: ▪ Book 5:	☐ IG ☐ FB ☐ TikTok ☐ BlueSky ☐ Threads ☐ YT ☐ Blog ☐ Other _____	☐ Research ☐ Prepare entry ☐ Submit _____

Date	Primary Book Progress	Other Books & Tasks	Social Media	Contests & Promos
Mon Mar 23	Words/pages: _____	Book 2: Book 3: Book 4: Book 5:	☐ IG ☐ FB ☐ TikTok ☐ BlueSky ☐ Threads ☐ YT ☐ Blog ☐ Other _____	☐ Research ☐ Prepare entry ☐ Submit _____
Tue Mar 24	Words/pages: _____	Book 2: Book 3: Book 4: Book 5:	☐ IG ☐ FB ☐ TikTok ☐ BlueSky ☐ Threads ☐ YT ☐ Blog ☐ Other _____	☐ Research ☐ Prepare entry ☐ Submit _____
Wed Mar 25	Words/pages: _____	Book 2: Book 3: Book 4: Book 5:	☐ IG ☐ FB ☐ TikTok ☐ BlueSky ☐ Threads ☐ YT ☐ Blog ☐ Other Prompt: ☐ March word count goal check-in _____	☐ Research ☐ Prepare entry ☐ Submit _____

Date	Primary Book Progress	Other Books & Tasks	Social Media	Contests & Promos
Thu Mar 26	Words/pages: _____	▨ Book 2: ▨ Book 3: ▨ Book 4: ▨ Book 5:	☐ IG ☐ FB ☐ TikTok ☐ BlueSky ☐ Threads ☐ YT ☐ Blog ☐ Other _____	☐ Research ☐ Prepare entry ☐ Submit _____
Fri Mar 27	Words/pages: _____	▨ Book 2: ▨ Book 3: ▨ Book 4: ▨ Book 5:	☐ IG ☐ FB ☐ TikTok ☐ BlueSky ☐ Threads ☐ YT ☐ Blog ☐ Other _____	☐ Research ☐ Prepare entry ☐ Submit _____
Sat Mar 28	Words/pages: _____	▨ Book 2: ▨ Book 3: ▨ Book 4: ▨ Book 5:	☐ IG ☐ FB ☐ TikTok ☐ BlueSky ☐ Threads ☐ YT ☐ Blog ☐ Other _____	☐ Research ☐ Prepare entry ☐ Submit _____

Date	Primary Book Progress	Other Books & Tasks	Social Media	Contests & Promos
Sun Mar 29	Words/pages: _____	Book 2: Book 3: Book 4: Book 5:	☐ IG ☐ FB ☐ TikTok ☐ BlueSky ☐ Threads ☐ YT ☐ Blog ☐ Other _____	☐ Research ☐ Prepare entry ☐ Submit _____
Mon Mar 30	Words/pages: _____	Book 2: Book 3: Book 4: Book 5:	☐ IG ☐ FB ☐ TikTok ☐ BlueSky ☐ Threads ☐ YT ☐ Blog ☐ Other _____	☐ Research ☐ Prepare entry ☐ Submit _____
Tue Mar 31	Words/pages: _____	Book 2: Book 3: Book 4: Book 5:	☐ IG ☐ FB ☐ TikTok ☐ BlueSky ☐ Threads ☐ YT ☐ Blog ☐ Other _____	☐ Research ☐ Prepare entry ☐ Submit _____

Notes:

_____

_____

_____

March Review & Reflection

Primary Book Progress:

Status: ☐ Completed ☐ In Progress ☐ On Hold

Words/Pages Written This Month: _____

Progress on Other Books:

Book 2:
_____

Book 3:
_____

Book 4:
_____

Book 5:
_____

What worked well this month:

_____

_____

_____

_____

Challenges and solutions:

_____

_____

_____

_____

Q1 2026

January - March

JANUARY

BOOK 1

Title:
_____

Genre:
_____

Status:
_____

BOOK 2

Title:
_____

Genre:
_____

Status:
_____

BOOK 3

Title:
_____

Genre:
_____

Status:
_____

FEBRUARY

BOOK 1

Title:
_____

Genre:
_____

Status:
_____

BOOK 2

Title:
_____

Genre:
_____

Status:
_____

BOOK 3

Title:
_____

Genre:
_____

Status:
_____

MARCH

BOOK 1

Title:
_____

Genre:
_____

Status:
_____

BOOK 2

Title:
_____

Genre:
_____

Status:
_____

BOOK 3

Title:
_____

Genre:
_____

Status:
_____

Q1 KEY DEADLINES & MILESTONES

_____
_____
_____
_____
_____
_____
_____
_____
_____
_____

Q1 REFLECTIONS & WINS

_____
_____
_____
_____
_____
_____

April 2026

Book to complete this month: _____

Genre: _____

Target Word/Page Count: _____

Current Stage: _____

Stage Guide:

- Planning - Outlining, research, character development

- Drafting - Active writing phase

- Revising - Content editing and restructuring

- Editing - Line editing and polishing

- Publishing Prep - Cover design, formatting, contest submissions

- Published - Promotion and marketing phase

Monthly Goals:

- Complete manuscript by day 21
- Finish editing and revisions by day 28
- Design professional cover
- Submit to at least 2 contests or promotional opportunities
- Post on social media 3x per week minimum
- _____
- _____

April 2026 - Projects Overview

Track up to 5 books in progress this month

Book	Title & Genre	Current Stage	Target Words/Pages	Month Goal
PRIMARY				
Book 2				
Book 3				
Book 4				
Book 5				

Book Color Coding Guide: Add highlighters or other shading for quick reference.

Book	Shading/Highlight Reference
PRIMARY (Book 1)	
Book 2	
Book 3	
Book 4	
Book 5	

April writing inspiration at a glance: **Add these to your calendar or tape them to your computer or wherever they will inspire you.**

April 1	April 2
"We should write because writing brings clarity and passion to the act of living." — Elie Wiesel	*"Better to write for yourself and have no public, than to write for the public and have no self."* — Cyril Connolly
April 3 *"The artist's only responsibility is to their art. They will be completely ruthless if they are good ones."* — James Baldwin	**April 4** *"A serious writer is not to be confounded with a solemn writer. A serious writer may be a hawk or a buzzard or even a popinjay, but a solemn writer is always a bloody owl."* — Ernest Hemingway
April 5 *"Write the book you want to read, the one you cannot find."* — Carol Shields	**April 6** *"I write because I have an innate need to write and create; to order the chaos of my experiences."* — bell hooks
April 7 *"The act of writing is an act of optimism. You wouldn't write if you didn't believe someone would read it."* — Edward Albee	**April 8** *"Writing is an exploration. You start from nothing and learn as you go."* — E.L. Doctorow

107

April 9
"The only way to learn to write is to force yourself to produce a certain number of words on a regular basis."
— William Zinsser

April 10
"I write because I am alone and I move through the world alone. No one will know what has passed through me."
— Nicole Krauss

April 11
"If you do not breathe through writing, if you do not cry out in writing, or sing in writing, then don't write."
— Anaïs Nin

April 13
"What is written without effort is in general read without pleasure."
— Samuel Johnson

April 12
"Writing is thinking. To write well is to think clearly. That's why it's so hard."
— David McCullough

April 14
"There are three rules for writing a novel. Unfortunately, no one knows what they are."
— W. Somerset Maugham

April 15
"You should write because you love the shape of stories and sentences and the creation of different words on a page."
— Annie Proulx

April 16
"Write your story as it needs to be written. Write it honestly, and tell it as best you can."
— Neil Gaiman

April 17
"The writer's only responsibility is to their art."
— William Faulkner

April 18
"Good writing is supposed to evoke sensation in the reader— not the fact that it is raining, but the feeling of being rained upon."
— E.L. Doctorow

April 19

"Writing is an act of faith, not a trick of grammar."
— E.B. White

April 20

"I am seeking. I am striving. I am in it with all my heart."
— Vincent van Gogh

April 21

"Writing is utter solitude, the descent into the cold abyss of oneself."
— Franz Kafka

April 22

"I try to create sympathy for my characters, then turn the monsters loose."
— Stephen King

April 23

"Writing saved me from the sin and inconvenience of violence."
— Alice Walker

April 24

"Don't wait for the muse. She has a lousy work ethic. Writers just write."
— Barbara Kingsolver

April 25

"The worst enemy to creativity is self-doubt."
— Sylvia Plath

April 26

"The scariest thing about writing is that you must tell the truth."
— Erica Jong

April 27

"A writer is someone for whom writing is more difficult than it is for other people."
— Thomas Mann

April 28

"If you're going to be a writer, the first essential is just to write. Do not wait for an idea. Start writing something."
— Wole Soyinka

April 29

"I write to make peace with the things I cannot control."
— Chimamanda Ngozi Adichie

April 30

"The story is what matters. The words are just the vehicle to get you there."
— Jhumpa Lahiri

April Social Media Planning

Monthly Social Media Goals & Tracking

Platform	Goal Posts	Completed	Content Ideas / Notes
Instagram	____	____	
Facebook	____	____	
TikTok	____	____	
BlueSky	____	____	
Threads	____	____	
LinkedIn	____	____	
YouTube/Shorts	____	____	
Pinterest	____	____	
Goodreads	____	____	
BookBub	____	____	
Author Website/Blog	____	____	

Weekly Social Media Content Calendar:

- Week 1: Behind-the-scenes character/plot development
- Week 2: Writing progress updates, word count milestones
- Week 3: First draft completion celebration, cover reveals

- Week 4: Book announcement, pre-order/launch details, contest entries

April Contest & Promotional Opportunities

Track submissions and deadlines

Contest/Opportunity	Deadline	Status	Entry Fee	Notes/Requirements
		☐ Plan ☐ Submit ☐ Done	$_____	
		☐ Plan ☐ Submit ☐ Done	$_____	
		☐ Plan ☐ Submit ☐ Done	$_____	
		☐ Plan ☐ Submit ☐ Done	$_____	
		☐ Plan ☐ Submit ☐ Done	$_____	
		☐ Plan ☐ Submit ☐ Done	$_____	
		☐ Plan ☐ Submit ☐ Done	$_____	
		☐ Plan ☐ Submit ☐ Done	$_____	
		☐ Plan ☐ Submit ☐ Done	$_____	
		☐ Plan ☐ Submit ☐ Done	$_____	

Promotional Opportunities Checklist:

- ☐ Book review blogs and websites
- ☐ BookTok/Bookstagram influencer outreach
- ☐ Goodreads giveaway or promotion
- ☐ BookBub featured deal submission
- ☐ Amazon/KDP advertising campaign
- ☐ Author newsletter announcement
- ☐ Podcast interview pitches
- ☐ Local bookstore/library events
- ☐ Cross-promotion with other authors
- ☐ Book club outreach

Stage Guide:

- Planning - Outlining, research, character development
- Drafting - Active writing phase
- Revising - Content editing and restructuring
- Editing - Line editing and polishing
- Publishing Prep - Cover design, formatting, contest submissions
- Published - Promotion and marketing phase

Week 1 (April 1-7): Writing Week

Primary Book Weekly Task Checklist:

PLANNING & SETUP (Days 1-3):

- ☐ Develop main characters (names, traits, motivations, arcs)
- ☐ Create basic plot outline or beat sheet
- ☐ Define key settings and world-building elements
- ☐ Research any necessary details for authenticity

WRITING BEGINS (Days 4-7):

- ☐ Write opening chapters (aim for 25% of target word count)
- ☐ Daily word/page count goal: _____ words/pages per day
- ☐ Establish narrative voice and tone
- ☐ Research 2-3 potential contests to enter

Date	Primary Book Progress	Other Books & Tasks	Social Media	Contests & Promos
Wed Apr 1	Words/pages: _____	Book 2: Book 3: Book 4: Book 5:	☐ IG ☐ FB ☐ TikTok ☐ BlueSky ☐ Threads ☐ YT ☐ Blog ☐ Other _____	☐ Research ☐ Prepare entry ☐ Submit _____

Date	Primary Book Progress	Other Books & Tasks	Social Media	Contests & Promos
Thu Apr 2	Words/pages: _____	Book 2: Book 3: Book 4: Book 5:	☐ IG ☐ FB ☐ TikTok ☐ BlueSky ☐ Threads ☐ YT ☐ Blog ☐ Other _____	☐ Research ☐ Prepare entry ☐ Submit _____
Fri Apr 3	Words/pages: _____	Book 2: Book 3: Book 4: Book 5:	☐ IG ☐ FB ☐ TikTok ☐ BlueSky ☐ Threads ☐ YT ☐ Blog ☐ Other Prompt: ☐ How I've grown as a writer_____ _____	☐ Research ☐ Prepare entry ☐ Submit _____
Sat Apr 4	Words/pages: _____	Book 2: Book 3: Book 4: Book 5:	☐ IG ☐ FB ☐ TikTok ☐ BlueSky ☐ Threads ☐ YT ☐ Blog ☐ Other _____	☐ Research ☐ Prepare entry ☐ Submit _____

Date	Primary Book Progress	Other Books & Tasks	Social Media	Contests & Promos
Sun Apr 5	Words/pages: _____	Book 2: Book 3: Book 4: Book 5:	☐ IG ☐ FB ☐ TikTok ☐ BlueSky ☐ Threads ☐ YT ☐ Blog ☐ Other _____	☐ Research ☐ Prepare entry ☐ Submit _____
Mon Apr 6	Words/pages: _____	Book 2: Book 3: Book 4: Book 5:	☐ IG ☐ FB ☐ TikTok ☐ BlueSky ☐ Threads ☐ YT ☐ Blog ☐ Other _____	☐ Research ☐ Prepare entry ☐ Submit _____
Tue Apr 7	Words/pages: _____	Book 2: Book 3: Book 4: Book 5:	☐ IG ☐ FB ☐ TikTok ☐ BlueSky ☐ Threads ☐ YT ☐ Blog ☐ Other Prompt: ☐ Lessons learned from failures _____	☐ Research ☐ Prepare entry ☐ Submit _____

Notes:

_____

_____

Week 2 (April 8-14): Writing Week

Primary Book Weekly Task Checklist:

INTENSIVE WRITING WEEK:

- ☐ Write middle section chapters (aim for 40-50% of total manuscript)
- ☐ Daily word/page count goal: _____ words/pages per day
- ☐ Build tension and develop character relationships
- ☐ Keep notes on continuity issues to fix later
- ☐ Don't edit yet - focus on getting words on the page

MARKETING PREP:

- ☐ Draft social media posts about your writing progress
- ☐ Start thinking about cover concepts

Date	Primary Book Progress	Other Books & Tasks	Social Media	Contests & Promos
Wed Apr 8	Words/pages: _____	Book 2: Book 3: Book 4: Book 5:	☐ IG ☐ FB ☐ TikTok ☐ BlueSky ☐ Threads ☐ YT ☐ Blog ☐ Other _____	☐ Research ☐ Prepare entry ☐ Submit _____

117

Date	Primary Book Progress	Other Books & Tasks	Social Media	Contests & Promos
Thu Apr 9	Words/pages: _____	Book 2: Book 3: Book 4: Book 5:	☐ IG ☐ FB ☐ TikTok ☐ BlueSky ☐ Threads ☐ YT ☐ Blog ☐ Other _____	☐ Research ☐ Prepare entry ☐ Submit _____
Fri Apr 10	Words/pages: _____	Book 2: Book 3: Book 4: Book 5:	☐ IG ☐ FB ☐ TikTok ☐ BlueSky ☐ Threads ☐ YT ☐ Blog ☐ Other _____	☐ Research ☐ Prepare entry ☐ Submit _____
Sat Apr 11	Words/pages: _____	Book 2: Book 3: Book 4: Book 5:	☐ IG ☐ FB ☐ TikTok ☐ BlueSky ☐ Threads ☐ YT ☐ Blog ☐ Other _____	☐ Research ☐ Prepare entry ☐ Submit _____

Date	Primary Book Progress	Other Books & Tasks	Social Media	Contests & Promos
Sun Apr 12	Words/pages: _____	Book 2: Book 3: Book 4: Book 5:	☐ IG ☐ FB ☐ TikTok ☐ BlueSky ☐ Threads ☐ YT ☐ Blog ☐ Other _____	☐ Research ☐ Prepare entry ☐ Submit _____
Mon Apr 13	Words/pages: _____	Book 2: Book 3: Book 4: Book 5:	☐ IG ☐ FB ☐ TikTok ☐ BlueSky ☐ Threads ☐ YT ☐ Blog ☐ Other Prompt: ☐ Editing process reveal _____	☐ Research ☐ Prepare entry ☐ Submit _____
Tue Apr 14	Words/pages: _____	Book 2: Book 3: Book 4: Book 5:	☐ IG ☐ FB ☐ TikTok ☐ BlueSky ☐ Threads ☐ YT ☐ Blog ☐ Other _____	☐ Research ☐ Prepare entry ☐ Submit _____

☐ **Keep notes on continuity issues to fix later**

_____
_____
_____
_____
_____
_____
_____
_____
_____
_____
_____
_____
_____
_____
_____

Week 3 (April 15-21): Writing Week

Primary Book Weekly Task Checklist:

FINISH FIRST DRAFT:

- ☐ Complete remaining chapters and conclusion
- ☐ Daily word/page count goal: _____ words/pages per day
- ☐ Write climax and resolution
- ☐ Ensure all plot threads are addressed
- ☐ Celebrate completing first draft!

PREPARATION FOR NEXT WEEK:

- ☐ Let manuscript rest for 1-2 days if possible
- ☐ Begin cover design research and mockups
- ☐ Finalize contest submission list

Date	Primary Book Progress	Other Books & Tasks	Social Media	Contests & Promos
Wed Apr 15	Words/pages: _____	Book 2: Book 3: Book 4: Book 5:	☐ IG ☐ FB ☐ TikTok ☐ BlueSky ☐ Threads ☐ YT ☐ Blog ☐ Other	☐ Research ☐ Prepare entry ☐ Submit _____

Date	Primary Book Progress	Other Books & Tasks	Social Media	Contests & Promos
Thu Apr 16	Words/pages: _____	Book 2: Book 3: Book 4: Book 5:	☐ IG ☐ FB ☐ TikTok ☐ BlueSky ☐ Threads ☐ YT ☐ Blog ☐ Other _____	☐ Research ☐ Prepare entry ☐ Submit _____
Fri Apr 17	Words/pages: _____	Book 2: Book 3: Book 4: Book 5:	☐ IG ☐ FB ☐ TikTok ☐ BlueSky ☐ Threads ☐ YT ☐ Blog ☐ Other _____	☐ Research ☐ Prepare entry ☐ Submit _____
Sat Apr 18	Words/pages: _____	Book 2: Book 3: Book 4: Book 5:	☐ IG ☐ FB ☐ TikTok ☐ BlueSky ☐ Threads ☐ YT ☐ Blog ☐ Other Prompt: ☐ Before/after: first draft vs. final _____	☐ Research ☐ Prepare entry ☐ Submit

Date	Primary Book Progress	Other Books & Tasks	Social Media	Contests & Promos
Sun Apr 19	Words/pages: _____	Book 2: Book 3: Book 4: Book 5:	☐ IG ☐ FB ☐ TikTok ☐ BlueSky ☐ Threads ☐ YT ☐ Blog ☐ Other _____	☐ Research ☐ Prepare entry ☐ Submit _____
Mon Apr 20	Words/pages: _____	Book 2: Book 3: Book 4: Book 5:	☐ IG ☐ FB ☐ TikTok ☐ BlueSky ☐ Threads ☐ YT ☐ Blog ☐ Other _____	☐ Research ☐ Prepare entry ☐ Submit _____
Tue Apr 21	Words/pages: _____	Book 2: Book 3: Book 4: Book 5:	☐ IG ☐ FB ☐ TikTok ☐ BlueSky ☐ Threads ☐ YT ☐ Blog ☐ Other _____	☐ Research ☐ Prepare entry ☐ Submit _____

Plot thread and/or cover design notes:

_____

_____

_____

Notes:

Week 4 (April 22-30): Editing & Publishing Week

Primary Book Weekly Task Checklist:

EDITING (Days 1-3):

- ☐ Read through entire manuscript, make notes
- ☐ Fix plot holes and continuity errors
- ☐ Strengthen weak scenes and dialogue
- ☐ Cut unnecessary content, tighten prose
- ☐ Proofread for grammar, spelling, typos

COVER & FORMATTING (Days 4-5):

- ☐ Design book cover (Canva, Photoshop, or hire designer)
- ☐ Format manuscript for publication (ebook/print)
- ☐ Write book description/blurb
- ☐ Create author bio if needed

PUBLISHING & PROMOTION (Days 6-9):

- ☐ Upload to publishing platform (KDP, IngramSpark, etc.)
- ☐ Submit to contest(s): _____
- ☐ Submit to contest(s): _____
- ☐ Schedule social media announcement posts
- ☐ Update author website/portfolio
- ☐ Send to beta readers or reviewers

125

Date	Primary Book Progress	Other Books & Tasks	Social Media	Contests & Promos
Wed Apr 22	Words/pages: _____	▪ Book 2: ▪ Book 3: ▪ Book 4: ▪ Book 5:	☐ IG ☐ FB ☐ TikTok ☐ BlueSky ☐ Threads ☐ YT ☐ Blog ☐ Other Prompt: ☐ National Poetry Month - share favorite poem _____	☐ Research ☐ Prepare entry ☐ Submit _____
Thu Apr 23	Words/pages: _____	▪ Book 2: ▪ Book 3: ▪ Book 4: ▪ Book 5:	☐ IG ☐ FB ☐ TikTok ☐ BlueSky ☐ Threads ☐ YT ☐ Blog ☐ Other _____	☐ Research ☐ Prepare entry ☐ Submit _____
Fri Apr 24	Words/pages: _____	▪ Book 2: ▪ Book 3: ▪ Book 4: ▪ Book 5:	☐ IG ☐ FB ☐ TikTok ☐ BlueSky ☐ Threads ☐ YT ☐ Blog ☐ Other _____	☐ Research ☐ Prepare entry ☐ Submit _____

Date	Primary Book Progress	Other Books & Tasks	Social Media	Contests & Promos
Sat Apr 25	Words/pages: _____	Book 2: Book 3: Book 4: Book 5:	☐ IG ☐ FB ☐ TikTok ☐ BlueSky ☐ Threads ☐ YT ☐ Blog ☐ Other _____	☐ Research ☐ Prepare entry ☐ Submit _____
Sun Apr 26	Words/pages: _____	Book 2: Book 3: Book 4: Book 5:	☐ IG ☐ FB ☐ TikTok ☐ BlueSky ☐ Threads ☐ YT ☐ Blog ☐ Other _____	☐ Research ☐ Prepare entry ☐ Submit _____
Mon Apr 27	Words/pages: _____	Book 2: Book 3: Book 4: Book 5:	☐ IG ☐ FB ☐ TikTok ☐ BlueSky ☐ Threads ☐ YT ☐ Blog ☐ Other _____	☐ Research ☐ Prepare entry ☐ Submit _____

Date	Primary Book Progress	Other Books & Tasks	Social Media	Contests & Promos
Tue Apr 28	Words/pages: _____	Book 2: Book 3: Book 4: Book 5:	☐ IG ☐ FB ☐ TikTok ☐ BlueSky ☐ Threads ☐ YT ☐ Blog ☐ Other _____	☐ Research ☐ Prepare entry ☐ Submit _____
Wed Apr 29	Words/pages: _____	Book 2: Book 3: Book 4: Book 5:	☐ IG ☐ FB ☐ TikTok ☐ BlueSky ☐ Threads ☐ YT ☐ Blog ☐ Other _____	☐ Research ☐ Prepare entry ☐ Submit _____
Thu Apr 30	Words/pages: _____	Book 2: Book 3: Book 4: Book 5:	☐ IG ☐ FB ☐ TikTok ☐ BlueSky ☐ Threads ☐ YT ☐ Blog ☐ Other Prompt: ☐ Spring book releases announcement _____	☐ Research ☐ Prepare entry ☐ Submit _____

Notes:

_____

_____

April Review & Reflection

Primary Book Progress:

Status: ☐ Completed ☐ In Progress ☐ On Hold

Words/Pages Written This Month: _____

Progress on Other Books:

Book 2:

_____

Book 3:

_____

Book 4:

_____

Book 5:

_____

What worked well this month:

_____

_____

_____

_____

Challenges and solutions:

_____

_____

_____

_____

May 2026

Book to complete this month: _____

Genre: _____

Target Word/Page Count: _____

Current Stage: _____

Stage Guide:

- Planning - Outlining, research, character development

- Drafting - Active writing phase

- Revising - Content editing and restructuring

- Editing - Line editing and polishing

- Publishing Prep - Cover design, formatting, contest submissions

- Published - Promotion and marketing phase

Monthly Goals:

- Complete manuscript by day 21
- Finish editing and revisions by day 28
- Design professional cover
- Submit to at least 2 contests or promotional opportunities
- Post on social media 3x per week minimum
- _____
- _____

May 2026 - Projects Overview

Track up to 5 books in progress this month

Book	Title & Genre	Current Stage	Target Words/Pages	Month Goal
PRIMARY				
Book 2				
Book 3				
Book 4				
Book 5				

Book Color Coding Guide: Add highlighters or other shading for quick reference.

Book	Shading/Highlight Reference
PRIMARY (Book 1)	
Book 2	
Book 3	
Book 4	
Book 5	

May writing inspiration at a glance: Add these to your calendar or tape them to your computer or wherever they will inspire you.

May 1 *"Writing is a concentrated form of thinking."* — Don DeLillo	**May 2** *"Books are a uniquely portable magic."* — Stephen King
May 3 *"I love writing. I love the swirl and swing of words as they tangle with human emotions."* — James A. Michener	**May 4** *"Writing is the painting of the voice."* — Voltaire
May 5 *"There is no greater agony than bearing an untold story inside you."* — Zora Neale Hurston	**May 6** *"Writing is like sex. First you do it for love, then you do it for your friends, and then you do it for money."* — Virginia Woolf
May 7 *"A writer who waits for ideal conditions under which to work will die without putting a word on paper."* — E.B. White	**May 8** *"I write differently from what I speak, I speak differently from what I think, I think differently from the way I ought to think."* — Franz Kafka
May 9 *"Your voice is important. Write it down. Read it aloud. Share it."* — Gloria E. Anzaldúa	**May 10** *"Fantasy is hardly an escape from reality. It's a way of understanding it."* — Lloyd Alexander

May 11

"To survive, you must tell stories."

— Umberto Eco

May 12

"I think all writing is a disease. You can't stop it."

— William Carlos Williams

May 13

"Writing is the only profession where no one considers you ridiculous if you earn no money."

— Jules Renard

May 14

"The pages are still blank, but there is a miraculous feeling of the words being there, written in invisible ink and clamoring to become visible."

— Vladimir Nabokov

May 15

"Writing is a form of personal freedom. It frees us from the mass identity we see in the making all around us."

— Don DeLillo

May 16

"The difference between fiction and reality? Fiction has to make sense."

— Tom Clancy

May 17

"Words are sacred. They deserve respect. If you get the right ones, in the right order, you can nudge the world a little."

— Tom Stoppard

May 18

"There is no rule on how to write. Sometimes it comes easily and perfectly; sometimes it's like drilling rock and then blasting it out with charges."

— Ernest Hemingway

May 19

"Writing is a rebellion against tyranny, and a fight for freedom."

— Arundhati Roy

May 20

"I believe that all good stories have a protagonist who is flawed."

— Gillian Flynn

May 21

"The more you read, the more things you will know. The more that you learn, the more places you'll go."
— Dr. Seuss

May 22

"Writing is the supreme solace."
— W. Somerset Maugham

May 23

"One must be drenched in words, literally soaked in them, to have the right ones form themselves into the proper pattern at the right moment."
— Hart Crane

May 24

"If you don't see the book you want on the shelf, write it."
— Beverly Cleary

May 25

"I write to record the truth of our lives."
— Roxane Gay

May 26

"Writing comes more easily if you have something to say."
— Sholem Asch

May 27

"There is nothing to writing. All you do is sit down at a typewriter and bleed."
— Ernest Hemingway

May 28

"A professional writer is an amateur who didn't quit."
— Richard Bach

May 29

"Write drunk, edit sober."
— Ernest Hemingway

May 30

"The writer must believe that what they are doing is the most important thing in the world. And they must hold to this illusion even when they know it is not true."
— John Steinbeck

May 31

"I paint myself because I am so often alone and because I am the subject I know best."
— Frida Kahlo

May Social Media Planning

Monthly Social Media Goals & Tracking

Platform	Goal Posts	Completed	Content Ideas / Notes
Instagram	_____	_____	
Facebook	_____	_____	
TikTok	_____	_____	
BlueSky	_____	_____	
Threads	_____	_____	
LinkedIn	_____	_____	
YouTube/Shorts	_____	_____	
Pinterest	_____	_____	
Goodreads	_____	_____	
BookBub	_____	_____	
Author Website/Blog	_____	_____	

Weekly Social Media Content Calendar:

- Week 1: Behind-the-scenes character/plot development
- Week 2: Writing progress updates, word count milestones
- Week 3: First draft completion celebration, cover reveals

- Week 4: Book announcement, pre-order/launch details, contest entries

May Contest & Promotional Opportunities

Track submissions and deadlines

Contest/Opportunity	Deadline	Status	Entry Fee	Notes/Requirements
		☐ Plan ☐ Submit ☐ Done	$_____	
		☐ Plan ☐ Submit ☐ Done	$_____	
		☐ Plan ☐ Submit ☐ Done	$_____	
		☐ Plan ☐ Submit ☐ Done	$_____	
		☐ Plan ☐ Submit ☐ Done	$_____	
		☐ Plan ☐ Submit ☐ Done	$_____	
		☐ Plan ☐ Submit ☐ Done	$_____	
		☐ Plan ☐ Submit ☐ Done	$_____	
		☐ Plan ☐ Submit ☐ Done	$_____	
		☐ Plan ☐ Submit ☐ Done	$_____	

Promotional Opportunities Checklist:

- ☐ Book review blogs and websites
- ☐ BookTok/Bookstagram influencer outreach
- ☐ Goodreads giveaway or promotion
- ☐ BookBub featured deal submission
- ☐ Amazon/KDP advertising campaign
- ☐ Author newsletter announcement
- ☐ Podcast interview pitches
- ☐ Local bookstore/library events
- ☐ Cross-promotion with other authors
- ☐ Book club outreach

Stage Guide:

- Planning - Outlining, research, character development
- Drafting - Active writing phase
- Revising - Content editing and restructuring
- Editing - Line editing and polishing
- Publishing Prep - Cover design, formatting, contest submissions
- Published - Promotion and marketing phase

Week 1 (May 1-7): Writing Week

Primary Book Weekly Task Checklist:

PLANNING & SETUP (Days 1-3):

- ☐ Develop main characters (names, traits, motivations, arcs)
- ☐ Create basic plot outline or beat sheet
- ☐ Define key settings and world-building elements
- ☐ Research any necessary details for authenticity

WRITING BEGINS (Days 4-7):

- ☐ Write opening chapters (aim for 25% of target word count)
- ☐ Daily word/page count goal: _____ words/pages per day
- ☐ Establish narrative voice and tone
- ☐ Research 2-3 potential contests to enter

Date	Primary Book Progress	Other Books & Tasks	Social Media	Contests & Promos
Fri May 1	Words/pages: _____	Book 2: Book 3: Book 4: Book 5:	☐ IG ☐ FB ☐ TikTok ☐ BlueSky ☐ Threads ☐ YT ☐ Blog ☐ Other Prompt: ☐ Celebrate completed manuscript _____	☐ Research ☐ Prepare entry ☐ Submit _____

Date	Primary Book Progress	Other Books & Tasks	Social Media	Contests & Promos
Sat May 2	Words/pages: _____	Book 2: Book 3: Book 4: Book 5:	☐ IG ☐ FB ☐ TikTok ☐ BlueSky ☐ Threads ☐ YT ☐ Blog ☐ Other _____	☐ Research ☐ Prepare entry ☐ Submit _____
Sun May 3	Words/pages: _____	Book 2: Book 3: Book 4: Book 5:	☐ IG ☐ FB ☐ TikTok ☐ BlueSky ☐ Threads ☐ YT ☐ Blog ☐ Other _____	☐ Research ☐ Prepare entry ☐ Submit _____
Mon May 4	Words/pages: _____	Book 2: Book 3: Book 4: Book 5:	☐ IG ☐ FB ☐ TikTok ☐ BlueSky ☐ Threads ☐ YT ☐ Blog ☐ Other _____	☐ Research ☐ Prepare entry ☐ Submit _____

Date	Primary Book Progress	Other Books & Tasks	Social Media	Contests & Promos
Tue May 5	Words/pages: _____	Book 2: Book 3: Book 4: Book 5:	☐ IG ☐ FB ☐ TikTok ☐ BlueSky ☐ Threads ☐ YT ☐ Blog ☐ Other _____	☐ Research ☐ Prepare entry ☐ Submit _____
Wed May 6	Words/pages: _____	Book 2: Book 3: Book 4: Book 5:	☐ IG ☐ FB ☐ TikTok ☐ BlueSky ☐ Threads ☐ YT ☐ Blog ☐ Other _____	☐ Research ☐ Prepare entry ☐ Submit _____
Thu May 7	Words/pages: _____	Book 2: Book 3: Book 4: Book 5:	☐ IG ☐ FB ☐ TikTok ☐ BlueSky ☐ Threads ☐ YT ☐ Blog ☐ Other _____	☐ Research ☐ Prepare entry ☐ Submit _____

Notes:

_____

_____

_____

Week 2 (May 8-14): Writing Week

Primary Book Weekly Task Checklist:

INTENSIVE WRITING WEEK:

- ☐ Write middle section chapters (aim for 40-50% of total manuscript)
- ☐ Daily word/page count goal: _____ words/pages per day
- ☐ Build tension and develop character relationships
- ☐ Keep notes on continuity issues to fix later
- ☐ Don't edit yet - focus on getting words on the page

MARKETING PREP:

- ☐ Draft social media posts about your writing progress
- ☐ Start thinking about cover concepts

Date	Primary Book Progress	Other Books & Tasks	Social Media	Contests & Promos
Fri May 8	Words/pages: _____	Book 2: Book 3: Book 4: Book 5:	☐ IG ☐ FB ☐ TikTok ☐ BlueSky ☐ Threads ☐ YT ☐ Blog ☐ Other Prompt: ☐ Writing anniversary (years writing)	☐ Research ☐ Prepare entry ☐ Submit _____

Date	Primary Book Progress	Other Books & Tasks	Social Media	Contests & Promos
Sat May 9	Words/pages: _____	▪ Book 2: ▪ Book 3: ▪ Book 4: ▪ Book 5:	□ IG □ FB □ TikTok □ BlueSky □ Threads □ YT □ Blog □ Other _____	□ Research □ Prepare entry □ Submit _____
Sun May 10	Words/pages: _____	▪ Book 2: ▪ Book 3: ▪ Book 4: ▪ Book 5:	□ IG □ FB □ TikTok □ BlueSky □ Threads □ YT □ Blog □ Other Prompt: □ Bookish Mother's Day content	□ Research □ Prepare entry □ Submit _____
Mon May 11	Words/pages: _____	▪ Book 2: ▪ Book 3: ▪ Book 4: ▪ Book 5:	□ IG □ FB □ TikTok □ BlueSky □ Threads □ YT □ Blog □ Other _____	□ Research □ Prepare entry □ Submit _____

Date	Primary Book Progress	Other Books & Tasks	Social Media	Contests & Promos
Tue May 12	Words/pages: _____	Book 2: Book 3: Book 4: Book 5:	☐ IG ☐ FB ☐ TikTok ☐ BlueSky ☐ Threads ☐ YT ☐ Blog ☐ Other _____	☐ Research ☐ Prepare entry ☐ Submit _____
Wed May 13	Words/pages: _____	Book 2: Book 3: Book 4: Book 5:	☐ IG ☐ FB ☐ TikTok ☐ BlueSky ☐ Threads ☐ YT ☐ Blog ☐ Other _____	☐ Research ☐ Prepare entry ☐ Submit _____
Thu May 14	Words/pages: _____	Book 2: Book 3: Book 4: Book 5:	☐ IG ☐ FB ☐ TikTok ☐ BlueSky ☐ Threads ☐ YT ☐ Blog ☐ Other _____	☐ Research ☐ Prepare entry ☐ Submit _____

☐ **Keep notes on continuity issues to fix later**

_____

_____

_____

Week 3 (May 15-21): Writing Week

Primary Book Weekly Task Checklist:

FINISH FIRST DRAFT:

- ☐ Complete remaining chapters and conclusion
- ☐ Daily word/page count goal: _____ words/pages per day
- ☐ Write climax and resolution
- ☐ Ensure all plot threads are addressed
- ☐ Celebrate completing first draft!

PREPARATION FOR NEXT WEEK:

- ☐ Let manuscript rest for 1-2 days if possible
- ☐ Begin cover design research and mockups
- ☐ Finalize contest submission list

Date	Primary Book Progress	Other Books & Tasks	Social Media	Contests & Promos
Fri May 15	Words/pages: _____	Book 2: Book 3: Book 4: Book 5:	☐ IG ☐ FB ☐ TikTok ☐ BlueSky ☐ Threads ☐ YT ☐ Blog ☐ Other Prompt: ☐ Behind-the-scenes: cover reveal prep	☐ Research ☐ Prepare entry ☐ Submit _____

149

Date	Primary Book Progress	Other Books & Tasks	Social Media	Contests & Promos
Sat May 16	Words/pages: _____	Book 2: Book 3: Book 4: Book 5:	☐ IG ☐ FB ☐ TikTok ☐ BlueSky ☐ Threads ☐ YT ☐ Blog ☐ Other _____	☐ Research ☐ Prepare entry ☐ Submit
Sun May 17	Words/pages: _____	Book 2: Book 3: Book 4: Book 5:	☐ IG ☐ FB ☐ TikTok ☐ BlueSky ☐ Threads ☐ YT ☐ Blog ☐ Other _____	☐ Research ☐ Prepare entry ☐ Submit _____
Mon May 18	Words/pages: _____	Book 2: Book 3: Book 4: Book 5:	☐ IG ☐ FB ☐ TikTok ☐ BlueSky ☐ Threads ☐ YT ☐ Blog ☐ Other _____	☐ Research ☐ Prepare entry ☐ Submit _____

Date	Primary Book Progress	Other Books & Tasks	Social Media	Contests & Promos
Tue May 19	Words/pages: _____	Book 2: Book 3: Book 4: Book 5:	☐ IG ☐ FB ☐ TikTok ☐ BlueSky ☐ Threads ☐ YT ☐ Blog ☐ Other _____	☐ Research ☐ Prepare entry ☐ Submit
Wed May 20	Words/pages: _____	Book 2: Book 3: Book 4: Book 5:	☐ IG ☐ FB ☐ TikTok ☐ BlueSky ☐ Threads ☐ YT ☐ Blog ☐ Other _____	☐ Research ☐ Prepare entry ☐ Submit _____
Thu May 21	Words/pages: _____	Book 2: Book 3: Book 4: Book 5:	☐ IG ☐ FB ☐ TikTok ☐ BlueSky ☐ Threads ☐ YT ☐ Blog ☐ Other Prompt: ☐ Writing mentor appreciation _____	☐ Research ☐ Prepare entry ☐ Submit

Plot thread and/or cover design notes:

_____

_____

Notes:

Week 4 (May 22-31): Editing & Publishing Week

Primary Book Weekly Task Checklist:

EDITING (Days 1-3):

- ☐ Read through entire manuscript, make notes
- ☐ Fix plot holes and continuity errors
- ☐ Strengthen weak scenes and dialogue
- ☐ Cut unnecessary content, tighten prose
- ☐ Proofread for grammar, spelling, typos

COVER & FORMATTING (Days 4-5):

- ☐ Design book cover (Canva, Photoshop, or hire designer)
- ☐ Format manuscript for publication (ebook/print)
- ☐ Write book description/blurb
- ☐ Create author bio if needed

PUBLISHING & PROMOTION (Days 6-10):

- ☐ Upload to publishing platform (KDP, IngramSpark, etc.)
- ☐ Submit to contest(s): _____
- ☐ Submit to contest(s): _____
- ☐ Schedule social media announcement posts
- ☐ Update author website/portfolio
- ☐ Send to beta readers or reviewers

Date	Primary Book Progress	Other Books & Tasks	Social Media	Contests & Promos
Fri May 22	Words/pages: _____	Book 2: Book 3: Book 4: Book 5:	☐ IG ☐ FB ☐ TikTok ☐ BlueSky ☐ Threads ☐ YT ☐ Blog ☐ Other _____	☐ Research ☐ Prepare entry ☐ Submit _____

Date	Primary Book Progress	Other Books & Tasks	Social Media	Contests & Promos
Sat May 23	Words/pages: _____	Book 2: Book 3: Book 4: Book 5:	☐ IG ☐ FB ☐ TikTok ☐ BlueSky ☐ Threads ☐ YT ☐ Blog ☐ Other Prompt: ☐ Memorial Day reading recommendations	☐ Research ☐ Prepare entry ☐ Submit _____
Sun May 24	Words/pages: _____	Book 2: Book 3: Book 4: Book 5:	☐ IG ☐ FB ☐ TikTok ☐ BlueSky ☐ Threads ☐ YT ☐ Blog ☐ Other _____	☐ Research ☐ Prepare entry ☐ Submit _____
Mon May 25	Words/pages: _____	Book 2: Book 3: Book 4: Book 5:	☐ IG ☐ FB ☐ TikTok ☐ BlueSky ☐ Threads ☐ YT ☐ Blog ☐ Other _____	☐ Research ☐ Prepare entry ☐ Submit _____

Date	Primary Book Progress	Other Books & Tasks	Social Media	Contests & Promos
Tue May 26	Words/pages: _____	Book 2: Book 3: Book 4: Book 5:	☐ IG ☐ FB ☐ TikTok ☐ BlueSky ☐ Threads ☐ YT ☐ Blog ☐ Other _____	☐ Research ☐ Prepare entry ☐ Submit _____
Wed May 27	Words/pages: _____	Book 2: Book 3: Book 4: Book 5:	☐ IG ☐ FB ☐ TikTok ☐ BlueSky ☐ Threads ☐ YT ☐ Blog ☐ Other _____	☐ Research ☐ Prepare entry ☐ Submit _____
Thu May 28	Words/pages: _____	Book 2: Book 3: Book 4: Book 5:	☐ IG ☐ FB ☐ TikTok ☐ BlueSky ☐ Threads ☐ YT ☐ Blog ☐ Other _____	☐ Research ☐ Prepare entry ☐ Submit _____

Date	Primary Book Progress	Other Books & Tasks	Social Media	Contests & Promos
Fri May 29	Words/pages: _____	Book 2: Book 3: Book 4: Book 5:	☐ IG ☐ FB ☐ TikTok ☐ BlueSky ☐ Threads ☐ YT ☐ Blog ☐ Other _____	☐ Research ☐ Prepare entry ☐ Submit
Sat May 30	Words/pages: _____	Book 2: Book 3: Book 4: Book 5:	☐ IG ☐ FB ☐ TikTok ☐ BlueSky ☐ Threads ☐ YT ☐ Blog ☐ Other _____	☐ Research ☐ Prepare entry ☐ Submit _____
Sun May 31	Words/pages: _____	Book 2: Book 3: Book 4: Book 5:	☐ IG ☐ FB ☐ TikTok ☐ BlueSky ☐ Threads ☐ YT ☐ Blog ☐ Other _____	☐ Research ☐ Prepare entry ☐ Submit _____

Notes:

_____

_____

_____

Designed by Jody Ortiz

May Review & Reflection

Primary Book Progress:

Status: ☐ Completed ☐ In Progress ☐ On Hold

Words/Pages Written This Month: _____

Progress on Other Books:

Book 2:
_____

Book 3:
_____

Book 4:
_____

Book 5:
_____

What worked well this month:

_____

_____

_____

_____

Challenges and solutions:

_____

_____

_____

_____

June 2026

Book to complete this month: _____

Genre: _____

Target Word/Page Count: _____

Current Stage: _____

Stage Guide:

- Planning - Outlining, research, character development

- Drafting - Active writing phase

- Revising - Content editing and restructuring

- Editing - Line editing and polishing

- Publishing Prep - Cover design, formatting, contest submissions

- Published - Promotion and marketing phase

Monthly Goals:

- Complete manuscript by day 21
- Finish editing and revisions by day 28
- Design professional cover
- Submit to at least 2 contests or promotional opportunities
- Post on social media 3x per week minimum
- _____
- _____

June 2026 - Projects Overview

Track up to 5 books in progress this month

Book	Title & Genre	Current Stage	Target Words/Pages	Month Goal
PRIMARY				
Book 2				
Book 3				
Book 4				
Book 5				

Book Color Coding Guide: Add highlighters or other shading for quick reference.

Book	Shading/Highlight Reference
PRIMARY (Book 1)	
Book 2	
Book 3	
Book 4	
Book 5	

June writing inspiration at a glance: Add these to your calendar or tape them to your computer or wherever they will inspire you.

June 1	June 2
"If you tell the truth, you don't have to remember anything." — Mark Twain	*"Every writer I know has trouble writing."* — Joseph Heller
June 3	**June 4**
"One day I will find the right words, and they will be simple." — Jack Kerouac	*"You must keep sending work out; you must never let a manuscript do nothing but eat its head off in a drawer."* — Isaac Asimov
June 5	**June 6**
"I write because I believe in the possibility of change." — Audre Lorde	*"Writing a novel is like driving a car at night. You can only see as far as your headlights, but you can make the whole trip that way."* — E.L. Doctorow
June 7	**June 8**
"The first sentence can't be written until the final sentence is written." — Joyce Carol Oates	*"The unread story is not a story; it is little black marks on wood pulp. The reader, reading it, makes it live."* — Ursula K. Le Guin
June 9	**June 10**
"A writer is a world trapped in a person." — Victor Hugo	*"Write with the door closed, rewrite with the door open."* — Stephen King

June 11

"Don't try to figure out what other people want to hear from you; figure out what you have to say."

— Barbara Kingsolver

June 12

"Writing is the geometry of the soul."

— Plato

June 13

"I can be changed by what happens to me. But I refuse to be reduced by it."

— Maya Angelou

June 14

"Any word you have to hunt for in a thesaurus is the wrong word."

— Stephen King

June 15

"Write only if you cannot live without writing. Write only what you alone can write."

— Elie Wiesel

June 16

"The thing all writers do best is find ways to avoid writing."

— Alan Dean Foster

June 17

"Writing is an act of hope."

— Isabel Allende

June 18

"A blank page is God's way of showing you how hard it is to be God."

— Unknown

June 19

"Writing is a solitary occupation. Family, friends, and society are the natural enemies of the writer."

— William Styron

June 20

"A writer's job is to tell the truth."

— Andy Rooney

June 21

"The only way out is through."

— Robert Frost

June 22

"I write because I must. It's not a choice or a pastime, it's an unyielding calling."

— Elizabeth Gilbert

June 23

"We write to expose the unexposed."
— Ta-Nehisi Coates

June 24

"Creativity is intelligence having fun."
— Albert Einstein

June 25

"Don't tell me what was said, show me the action."
— Anton Chekhov

June 26

"One thing that helps is to give myself permission to write badly. I tell myself that I'm going to do my five or ten pages no matter what."
— Sandra Cisneros

June 27

"Writers are not just people who sit down and write. They hazard themselves."
— Edna O'Brien

June 28

"Writing is a necessity and an addiction and a solace."
— Jamaica Kincaid

June 29

"The purpose of writing is to inflate weak ideas, obscure pure reasoning, and inhibit clarity."
— Bill Watterson

June 30

"Great writers are indecent people, they live unfairly, saving the best part for paper."
— Anaïs Nin

June Social Media Planning

Monthly Social Media Goals & Tracking

Platform	Goal Posts	Completed	Content Ideas / Notes
Instagram	____	____	
Facebook	____	____	
TikTok	____	____	
BlueSky	____	____	
Threads	____	____	
LinkedIn	____	____	
YouTube/Shorts	____	____	
Pinterest	____	____	
Goodreads	____	____	
BookBub	____	____	
Author Website/Blog	____	____	

Weekly Social Media Content Calendar:

- Week 1: Behind-the-scenes character/plot development
- Week 2: Writing progress updates, word count milestones
- Week 3: First draft completion celebration, cover reveals

- Week 4: Book announcement, pre-order/launch details, contest entries

June Contest & Promotional Opportunities

Track submissions and deadlines

Contest/Opportunity	Deadline	Status	Entry Fee	Notes/Requirements
		☐ Plan ☐ Submit ☐ Done	$_____	
		☐ Plan ☐ Submit ☐ Done	$_____	
		☐ Plan ☐ Submit ☐ Done	$_____	
		☐ Plan ☐ Submit ☐ Done	$_____	
		☐ Plan ☐ Submit ☐ Done	$_____	
		☐ Plan ☐ Submit ☐ Done	$_____	
		☐ Plan ☐ Submit ☐ Done	$_____	
		☐ Plan ☐ Submit ☐ Done	$_____	
		☐ Plan ☐ Submit ☐ Done	$_____	
		☐ Plan ☐ Submit ☐ Done	$_____	

Promotional Opportunities Checklist:

- ☐ Book review blogs and websites
- ☐ BookTok/Bookstagram influencer outreach
- ☐ Goodreads giveaway or promotion
- ☐ BookBub featured deal submission
- ☐ Amazon/KDP advertising campaign
- ☐ Author newsletter announcement
- ☐ Podcast interview pitches
- ☐ Local bookstore/library events
- ☐ Cross-promotion with other authors
- ☐ Book club outreach

Stage Guide:

- Planning - Outlining, research, character development
- Drafting - Active writing phase
- Revising - Content editing and restructuring
- Editing - Line editing and polishing
- Publishing Prep - Cover design, formatting, contest submissions
- Published - Promotion and marketing phase

Week 1 (June 1-7): Writing Week

Primary Book Weekly Task Checklist:

PLANNING & SETUP (Days 1-3):

- ☐ Develop main characters (names, traits, motivations, arcs)
- ☐ Create basic plot outline or beat sheet
- ☐ Define key settings and world-building elements
- ☐ Research any necessary details for authenticity

WRITING BEGINS (Days 4-7):

- ☐ Write opening chapters (aim for 25% of target word count)
- ☐ Daily word/page count goal: _____ words/pages per day
- ☐ Establish narrative voice and tone
- ☐ Research 2-3 potential contests to enter

Date	Primary Book Progress	Other Books & Tasks	Social Media	Contests & Promos
Mon Jun 1	Words/pages: _____ ☐ Develop main characters (names, traits, motivations, arcs) ☐ Create basic plot outline or beat sheet ☐ Define key settings and world-building elements ☐ Research any necessary details for authenticity	Book 2: _____ Book 3: _____ Book 4: _____ Book 5: _____	☐ IG ☐ FB ☐ TikTok ☐ BlueSky ☐ Threads ☐ YT ☐ Blog ☐ Other _____ _____	☐ Research ☐ Prepare entry ☐ Submit _____ _____ _

Date	Primary Book Progress	Other Books & Tasks	Social Media	Contests & Promos
Tue Jun 2	Words/pages: _____	Book 2: Book 3: Book 4: Book 5:	☐ IG ☐ FB ☐ TikTok ☐ BlueSky ☐ Threads ☐ YT ☐ Blog ☐ Other _____	☐ Research ☐ Prepare entry ☐ Submit _____
Wed Jun 3	Words/pages: _____	Book 2: Book 3: Book 4: Book 5:	☐ IG ☐ FB ☐ TikTok ☐ BlueSky ☐ Threads ☐ YT ☐ Blog ☐ Other _____	☐ Research ☐ Prepare entry ☐ Submit _____
Thu Jun 4	Words/pages: _____	Book 2: Book 3: Book 4: Book 5:	☐ IG ☐ FB ☐ TikTok ☐ BlueSky ☐ Threads ☐ YT ☐ Blog ☐ Other _____	☐ Research ☐ Prepare entry ☐ Submit _____

Date	Primary Book Progress	Other Books & Tasks	Social Media	Contests & Promos
Fri Jun 5	Words/pages: _____	Book 2: Book 3: Book 4: Book 5:	☐ IG ☐ FB ☐ TikTok ☐ BlueSky ☐ Threads ☐ YT ☐ Blog ☐ Other Prompt: ☐ Perfect summer reads list	☐ Research ☐ Prepare entry ☐ Submit
Sat Jun 6	Words/pages: _____	Book 2: Book 3: Book 4: Book 5:	☐ IG ☐ FB ☐ TikTok ☐ BlueSky ☐ Threads ☐ YT ☐ Blog ☐ Other	☐ Research ☐ Prepare entry ☐ Submit
Sun Jun 7	Words/pages: _____	Book 2: Book 3: Book 4: Book 5:	☐ IG ☐ FB ☐ TikTok ☐ BlueSky ☐ Threads ☐ YT ☐ Blog ☐ Other	☐ Research ☐ Prepare entry ☐ Submit

Notes:

Week 2 (June 8-14): Writing Week

Primary Book Weekly Task Checklist:

INTENSIVE WRITING WEEK:

- ☐ Write middle section chapters (aim for 40-50% of total manuscript)
- ☐ Daily word/page count goal: _____ words/pages per day
- ☐ Build tension and develop character relationships
- ☐ Keep notes on continuity issues to fix later
- ☐ Don't edit yet - focus on getting words on the page

MARKETING PREP:

- ☐ Draft social media posts about your writing progress
- ☐ Start thinking about cover concepts

Date	Primary Book Progress	Other Books & Tasks	Social Media	Contests & Promos
Mon Jun 8	Words/pages: _____	Book 2: Book 3: Book 4: Book 5:	☐ IG ☐ FB ☐ TikTok ☐ BlueSky ☐ Threads ☐ YT ☐ Blog ☐ Other _____	☐ Research ☐ Prepare entry ☐ Submit _____

Date	Primary Book Progress	Other Books & Tasks	Social Media	Contests & Promos
Tue Jun 9	Words/pages: _____	Book 2: Book 3: Book 4: Book 5:	☐ IG ☐ FB ☐ TikTok ☐ BlueSky ☐ Threads ☐ YT ☐ Blog ☐ Other _____	☐ Research ☐ Prepare entry ☐ Submit _____
Wed Jun 10	Words/pages: _____	Book 2: Book 3: Book 4: Book 5:	☐ IG ☐ FB ☐ TikTok ☐ BlueSky ☐ Threads ☐ YT ☐ Blog ☐ Other _____	☐ Research ☐ Prepare entry ☐ Submit _____
Thu Jun 11	Words/pages: _____	Book 2: Book 3: Book 4: Book 5:	☐ IG ☐ FB ☐ TikTok ☐ BlueSky ☐ Threads ☐ YT ☐ Blog ☐ Other Prompt: ☐ Beach/vacation writing setup _____	☐ Research ☐ Prepare entry ☐ Submit _____

173

Date	Primary Book Progress	Other Books & Tasks	Social Media	Contests & Promos
Fri Jun 12	Words/pages: _____	Book 2: Book 3: Book 4: Book 5:	☐ IG ☐ FB ☐ TikTok ☐ BlueSky ☐ Threads ☐ YT ☐ Blog ☐ Other _____	☐ Research ☐ Prepare entry ☐ Submit _____
Sat Jun 13	Words/pages: _____	Book 2: Book 3: Book 4: Book 5:	☐ IG ☐ FB ☐ TikTok ☐ BlueSky ☐ Threads ☐ YT ☐ Blog ☐ Other Prompt: ☐ Summer-themed excerpt from books _____	☐ Research ☐ Prepare entry ☐ Submit _____
Sun Jun 14	Words/pages: _____	Book 2: Book 3: Book 4: Book 5:	☐ IG ☐ FB ☐ TikTok ☐ BlueSky ☐ Threads ☐ YT ☐ Blog ☐ Other _____	☐ Research ☐ Prepare entry ☐ Submit _____

☐ Keep notes on continuity issues to fix later

_____
_____
_____
_____
_____
_____
_____
_____
_____
_____
_____
_____
_____
_____
_____
_____
_____

Week 3 (June 15-21): Writing Week

Primary Book Weekly Task Checklist:

FINISH FIRST DRAFT:

- ☐ Complete remaining chapters and conclusion
- ☐ Daily word/page count goal: _____ words/pages per day
- ☐ Write climax and resolution
- ☐ Ensure all plot threads are addressed
- ☐ Celebrate completing first draft!

PREPARATION FOR NEXT WEEK:

- ☐ Let manuscript rest for 1-2 days if possible
- ☐ Begin cover design research and mockups
- ☐ Finalize contest submission list

Date	Primary Book Progress	Other Books & Tasks	Social Media	Contests & Promos
Mon Jun 15	Words/pages: _____	Book 2: Book 3: Book 4: Book 5:	☐ IG ☐ FB ☐ TikTok ☐ BlueSky ☐ Threads ☐ YT ☐ Blog ☐ Other Prompt: ☐ Pride Month: diverse books/charac ters _____	☐ Research ☐ Prepare entry ☐ Submit _____

Date	Primary Book Progress	Other Books & Tasks	Social Media	Contests & Promos
Tue Jun 16	Words/pages: _____	Book 2: Book 3: Book 4: Book 5:	☐ IG ☐ FB ☐ TikTok ☐ BlueSky ☐ Threads ☐ YT ☐ Blog ☐ Other _____	☐ Research ☐ Prepare entry ☐ Submit _____
Wed Jun 17	Words/pages: _____	Book 2: Book 3: Book 4: Book 5:	☐ IG ☐ FB ☐ TikTok ☐ BlueSky ☐ Threads ☐ YT ☐ Blog ☐ Other _____	☐ Research ☐ Prepare entry ☐ Submit _____
Thu Jun 18	Words/pages: _____	Book 2: Book 3: Book 4: Book 5:	☐ IG ☐ FB ☐ TikTok ☐ BlueSky ☐ Threads ☐ YT ☐ Blog ☐ Other Prompt: ☐ Father's Day book gift guide _____	☐ Research ☐ Prepare entry ☐ Submit _____

177

Date	Primary Book Progress	Other Books & Tasks	Social Media	Contests & Promos
Fri Jun 19	Words/pages: _____	Book 2: Book 3: Book 4: Book 5:	□ IG □ FB □ TikTok □ BlueSky □ Threads □ YT □ Blog □ Other _____	□ Research □ Prepare entry □ Submit
Sat Jun 20	Words/pages: _____	Book 2: Book 3: Book 4: Book 5:	□ IG □ FB □ TikTok □ BlueSky □ Threads □ YT □ Blog □ Other _____	□ Research □ Prepare entry □ Submit _____
Sun Jun 21	Words/pages: _____	Book 2: Book 3: Book 4: Book 5:	□ IG □ FB □ TikTok □ BlueSky □ Threads □ YT □ Blog □ Other _____	□ Research □ Prepare entry □ Submit _____

Plot thread and/or cover design notes:

_____

_____

_____

Notes:

Week 4 (June 22-30): Editing & Publishing Week

Primary Book Weekly Task Checklist:

EDITING (Days 1-3):

- ☐ Read through entire manuscript, make notes
- ☐ Fix plot holes and continuity errors
- ☐ Strengthen weak scenes and dialogue
- ☐ Cut unnecessary content, tighten prose
- ☐ Proofread for grammar, spelling, typos

COVER & FORMATTING (Days 4-5):

- ☐ Design book cover (Canva, Photoshop, or hire designer)
- ☐ Format manuscript for publication (ebook/print)
- ☐ Write book description/blurb
- ☐ Create author bio if needed

PUBLISHING & PROMOTION (Days 6-9):

- ☐ Upload to publishing platform (KDP, IngramSpark, etc.)
- ☐ Submit to contest(s): _____
- ☐ Submit to contest(s): _____
- ☐ Schedule social media announcement posts
- ☐ Update author website/portfolio
- ☐ Send to beta readers or reviewers

Date	Primary Book Progress	Other Books & Tasks	Social Media	Contests & Promos
Mon Jun 22	Words/pages: _____	Book 2: Book 3: Book 4: Book 5:	☐ IG ☐ FB ☐ TikTok ☐ BlueSky ☐ Threads ☐ YT ☐ Blog ☐ Other Prompt: ☐ Mid-year goals check-in _____	☐ Research ☐ Prepare entry ☐ Submit
Tue Jun 23	Words/pages: _____	Book 2: Book 3: Book 4: Book 5:	☐ IG ☐ FB ☐ TikTok ☐ BlueSky ☐ Threads ☐ YT ☐ Blog ☐ Other _____	☐ Research ☐ Prepare entry ☐ Submit _____
Wed Jun 24	Words/pages: _____	Book 2: Book 3: Book 4: Book 5:	☐ IG ☐ FB ☐ TikTok ☐ BlueSky ☐ Threads ☐ YT ☐ Blog ☐ Other _____	☐ Research ☐ Prepare entry ☐ Submit _____

181

Date	Primary Book Progress	Other Books & Tasks	Social Media	Contests & Promos
Thu Jun 25	Words/pages: _____	Book 2: Book 3: Book 4: Book 5:	☐ IG ☐ FB ☐ TikTok ☐ BlueSky ☐ Threads ☐ YT ☐ Blog ☐ Other _____	☐ Research ☐ Prepare entry ☐ Submit _____
Fri Jun 26	Words/pages: _____	Book 2: Book 3: Book 4: Book 5:	☐ IG ☐ FB ☐ TikTok ☐ BlueSky ☐ Threads ☐ YT ☐ Blog ☐ Other _____	☐ Research ☐ Prepare entry ☐ Submit _____
Sat Jun 27	Words/pages: _____	Book 2: Book 3: Book 4: Book 5:	☐ IG ☐ FB ☐ TikTok ☐ BlueSky ☐ Threads ☐ YT ☐ Blog ☐ Other _____	☐ Research ☐ Prepare entry ☐ Submit _____

Date	Primary Book Progress	Other Books & Tasks	Social Media	Contests & Promos
Sun Jun 28	Words/pages: _____	Book 2: Book 3: Book 4: Book 5:	☐ IG ☐ FB ☐ TikTok ☐ BlueSky ☐ Threads ☐ YT ☐ Blog ☐ Other _____	☐ Research ☐ Prepare entry ☐ Submit _____
Mon Jun 29	Words/pages: _____	Book 2: Book 3: Book 4: Book 5:	☐ IG ☐ FB ☐ TikTok ☐ BlueSky ☐ Threads ☐ YT ☐ Blog ☐ Other _____	☐ Research ☐ Prepare entry ☐ Submit _____
Tue Jun 30	Words/pages: _____	Book 2: Book 3: Book 4: Book 5:	☐ IG ☐ FB ☐ TikTok ☐ BlueSky ☐ Threads ☐ YT ☐ Blog ☐ Other _____	☐ Research ☐ Prepare entry ☐ Submit _____

Notes:

_____

_____

_____

183

June Review & Reflection

Primary Book Progress:

Status: ☐ Completed ☐ In Progress ☐ On Hold

Words/Pages Written This Month: _____

Progress on Other Books:

Book 2:
_____

Book 3:
_____

Book 4:
_____

Book 5:
_____

What worked well this month:

_____
_____
_____
_____

Challenges and solutions:

_____
_____
_____
_____

Q2 2026

April - June

APRIL

BOOK 1

Title:

_____

Genre:

_____

Status:

_____

BOOK 2

Title:

_____

Genre:

_____

Status:

_____

BOOK 3

Title:

_____

Genre:

_____

Status:

_____

MAY

BOOK 1

Title:

_____

Genre:

_____

Status:

_____

BOOK 2

Title:

_____

Genre:

_____

Status:

_____

BOOK 3

Title:

_____

Genre:

_____

Status:

_____

JUNE

BOOK 1

Title:

_____

Genre:

_____

Status:

_____

BOOK 2

Title:

_____

Genre:

_____

Status:

_____

BOOK 3

Title:

_____

Genre:

_____

Status:

_____

Q2 KEY DEADLINES & MILESTONES

_____

_____

_____

_____

_____

_____

_____

_____

_____

_____

_____

_____

Q2 REFLECTIONS & WINS

_____

_____

_____

_____

_____

_____

_____

July 2026

Book to complete this month: _____

Genre: _____

Target Word/Page Count: _____

Current Stage: _____

Stage Guide:

- Planning - Outlining, research, character development

- Drafting - Active writing phase

- Revising - Content editing and restructuring

- Editing - Line editing and polishing

- Publishing Prep - Cover design, formatting, contest submissions

- Published - Promotion and marketing phase

Monthly Goals:

- Complete manuscript by day 21
- Finish editing and revisions by day 28
- Design professional cover
- Submit to at least 2 contests or promotional opportunities
- Post on social media 3x per week minimum
- _____
- _____

July 2026 - Projects Overview

Track up to 5 books in progress this month

Book	Title & Genre	Current Stage	Target Words/Pages	Month Goal
PRIMARY				
Book 2				
Book 3				
Book 4				
Book 5				

Book Color Coding Guide: Add highlighters or other shading for quick reference.

Book	Shading/Highlight Reference
PRIMARY (Book 1)	
Book 2	
Book 3	
Book 4	
Book 5	

July writing inspiration at a glance: Add these to your calendar or tape them to your computer or wherever they will inspire you.

July 1	July 2
"The two most engaging powers of an author are to make new things familiar, familiar things new." — William Makepeace Thackeray	*"Find out the reason that commands you to write; see whether it has spread its roots into the very depth of your heart."* — Rainer Maria Rilke
July 3	**July 4**
"Writing is a craft, and a writer is a craftsperson." — Margaret Atwood	*"The art of writing is the art of discovering what you believe."* — Gustave Flaubert
July 5	**July 6**
"Not everything that can be counted counts, and not everything that counts can be counted." — Albert Einstein	*"Writing is the only thing that, when I do it, I don't feel I should be doing something else."* — Gloria Steinem
July 7	**July 8**
"Tell the story that only you can tell." — Cheryl Strayed	*"We do not write in order to be understood; we write in order to understand."* — C.S. Lewis
July 9	**July 10**
"Writing is my way of expressing—and thereby eliminating—all the various ways we can be wrong-headed." — Zadie Smith	*"Stories have to be told or they die, and when they die, we can't remember who we are or why we're here."* — Sue Monk Kidd

July 11

"Your story matters. Don't let anyone tell you otherwise."
— Jacqueline Woodson

July 12

"As a writer, you should not judge, you should understand."
— Ernest Hemingway

July 13

"Write the truest sentence you know."
— Ernest Hemingway

July 14

"You own everything that happened to you. Tell your stories."
— Anne Lamott

July 15

"I have always been delighted at the prospect of a new day, a fresh try, one more start, with perhaps a bit of magic waiting somewhere behind the morning."
— J.B. Priestley

July 16

"Writers are always selling somebody out."
— Joan Didion

July 17

"No one else sees the world the way you do, so no one else can tell the stories that you have to tell."
— Charles de Lint

July 18

"The beautiful thing about writing is that you don't have to wait for someone to give you permission to do it."
— Caitlin Moran

July 19

"You don't write because you want to say something, you write because you have something to say."
— F. Scott Fitzgerald

July 20

"Be yourself. Everyone else is already taken."
— Oscar Wilde

July 21

"How vain it is to sit down to write when you have not stood up to live."
— Henry David Thoreau

July 22

"Writing is like breathing, it's possible to learn to do it well, but the point is to do it no matter what."
— Julia Cameron

July 23

"The privilege of a lifetime is to become who you truly are."
— Carl Jung

July 24

"Writing is not about youth but about spark of imagination at any age."
— Darynda Jones

July 25

"Imagination is everything. It is the preview of life's coming attractions."
— Albert Einstein

July 26

"Writing becomes a spiritual practice when you commit to it fully."
— Natalie Goldberg

July 27

"Don't classify me, read me. I'm a writer, not a genre."
— Carlos Fuentes

July 28

"I believe in the power of the written word to change hearts and minds."
— Malala Yousafzai

July 29

"Story is just data with a soul."
— Brené Brown

July 30

"Your voice matters. Your story matters. Your words matter."

— Ijeoma Oluo

July 31

"The most important things are the hardest to say, because words diminish them."
— Stephen King

July Social Media Planning

Monthly Social Media Goals & Tracking

Platform	Goal Posts	Completed	Content Ideas / Notes
Instagram	____	____	
Facebook	____	____	
TikTok	____	____	
BlueSky	____	____	
Threads	____	____	
LinkedIn	____	____	
YouTube/Shorts	____	____	
Pinterest	____	____	
Goodreads	____	____	
BookBub	____	____	
Author Website/Blog	____	____	

Weekly Social Media Content Calendar:

- Week 1: Behind-the-scenes character/plot development
- Week 2: Writing progress updates, word count milestones
- Week 3: First draft completion celebration, cover reveals

- Week 4: Book announcement, pre-order/launch details, contest entries

July Contest & Promotional Opportunities

Track submissions and deadlines

Contest/Opportunity	Deadline	Status	Entry Fee	Notes/Requirements
		☐ Plan ☐ Submit ☐ Done	$_____	
		☐ Plan ☐ Submit ☐ Done	$_____	
		☐ Plan ☐ Submit ☐ Done	$_____	
		☐ Plan ☐ Submit ☐ Done	$_____	
		☐ Plan ☐ Submit ☐ Done	$_____	
		☐ Plan ☐ Submit ☐ Done	$_____	
		☐ Plan ☐ Submit ☐ Done	$_____	
		☐ Plan ☐ Submit ☐ Done	$_____	
		☐ Plan ☐ Submit ☐ Done	$_____	
		☐ Plan ☐ Submit ☐ Done	$_____	

Promotional Opportunities Checklist:

- ☐ Book review blogs and websites
- ☐ BookTok/Bookstagram influencer outreach
- ☐ Goodreads giveaway or promotion
- ☐ BookBub featured deal submission
- ☐ Amazon/KDP advertising campaign
- ☐ Author newsletter announcement
- ☐ Podcast interview pitches
- ☐ Local bookstore/library events
- ☐ Cross-promotion with other authors
- ☐ Book club outreach

Stage Guide:

- Planning - Outlining, research, character development
- Drafting - Active writing phase
- Revising - Content editing and restructuring
- Editing - Line editing and polishing
- Publishing Prep - Cover design, formatting, contest submissions
- Published - Promotion and marketing phase

Week 1 (July 1-7): Writing Week

Primary Book Weekly Task Checklist:

PLANNING & SETUP (Days 1-3):

- ☐ Develop main characters (names, traits, motivations, arcs)
- ☐ Create basic plot outline or beat sheet
- ☐ Define key settings and world-building elements
- ☐ Research any necessary details for authenticity

WRITING BEGINS (Days 4-7):

- ☐ Write opening chapters (aim for 25% of target word count)
- ☐ Daily word/page count goal: _____ words/pages day
- ☐ Establish narrative voice and tone
- ☐ Research 2-3 potential contests to enter

Date	Primary Book Progress	Other Books & Tasks	Social Media	Contests & Promos
Wed Jul 1	Words/pages: _____	Book 2: Book 3: Book 4: Book 5:	☐ IG ☐ FB ☐ TikTok ☐ BlueSky ☐ Threads ☐ YT ☐ Blog ☐ Other Prompt: ☐ Fireworks = plot twists metaphor	☐ Research ☐ Prepare entry ☐ Submit _____

Date	Primary Book Progress	Other Books & Tasks	Social Media	Contests & Promos
Thu Jul 2		Book 2: Book 3: Book 4: Book 5:	☐ IG ☐ FB ☐ TikTok ☐ BlueSky ☐ Threads ☐ YT ☐ Blog ☐ Other _____	☐ Research ☐ Prepare entry ☐ Submit _____
Fri Jul 3	Words/pages: _____	Book 2: Book 3: Book 4: Book 5:	☐ IG ☐ FB ☐ TikTok ☐ BlueSky ☐ Threads ☐ YT ☐ Blog ☐ Other _____	☐ Research ☐ Prepare entry ☐ Submit _____
Sat Jul 4	Words/pages: _____	Book 2: Book 3: Book 4: Book 5:	☐ IG ☐ FB ☐ TikTok ☐ BlueSky ☐ Threads ☐ YT ☐ Blog ☐ Other _____	☐ Research ☐ Prepare entry ☐ Submit _____

Date	Primary Book Progress	Other Books & Tasks	Social Media	Contests & Promos
Sun Jul 5	Words/pages: _____	Book 2: Book 3: Book 4: Book 5:	☐ IG ☐ FB ☐ TikTok ☐ BlueSky ☐ Threads ☐ YT ☐ Blog ☐ Other _____	☐ Research ☐ Prepare entry ☐ Submit _____
Mon Jul 6	Words/pages: _____	Book 2: Book 3: Book 4: Book 5:	☐ IG ☐ FB ☐ TikTok ☐ BlueSky ☐ Threads ☐ YT ☐ Blog ☐ Other Prompt: ☐ Why I chose _____. publishing	☐ Research ☐ Prepare entry ☐ Submit _____
Tue Jul 7	Words/pages: _____	Book 2: Book 3: Book 4: Book 5:	☐ IG ☐ FB ☐ TikTok ☐ BlueSky ☐ Threads ☐ YT ☐ Blog ☐ Other _____	☐ Research ☐ Prepare entry ☐ Submit _____

Notes:

Week 2 (July 8-14): Writing Week

Primary Book Weekly Task Checklist:

INTENSIVE WRITING WEEK:

- ☐ Write middle section chapters (aim for 40-50% of total manuscript)
- ☐ Daily word/page count goal: _____ words/pages per day
- ☐ Build tension and develop character relationships
- ☐ Keep notes on continuity issues to fix later
- ☐ Don't edit yet - focus on getting words on the page

MARKETING PREP:

- ☐ Draft social media posts about your writing progress
- ☐ Start thinking about cover concepts

Date	Primary Book Progress	Other Books & Tasks	Social Media	Contests & Promos
Wed Jul 8	Words/pages: _____	Book 2: Book 3: Book 4: Book 5:	☐ IG ☐ FB ☐ TikTok ☐ BlueSky ☐ Threads ☐ YT ☐ Blog ☐ Other _____	☐ Research ☐ Prepare entry ☐ Submit _____

Date	Primary Book Progress	Other Books & Tasks	Social Media	Contests & Promos
Thu Jul 9	Words/pages: _____	Book 2: Book 3: Book 4: Book 5:	☐ IG ☐ FB ☐ TikTok ☐ BlueSky ☐ Threads ☐ YT ☐ Blog ☐ Other _____	☐ Research ☐ Prepare entry ☐ Submit
Fri Jul 10	Words/pages: _____	Book 2: Book 3: Book 4: Book 5:	☐ IG ☐ FB ☐ TikTok ☐ BlueSky ☐ Threads ☐ YT ☐ Blog ☐ Other _____	☐ Research ☐ Prepare entry ☐ Submit _____
Sat Jul 11	Words/pages: _____	Book 2: Book 3: Book 4: Book 5:	☐ IG ☐ FB ☐ TikTok ☐ BlueSky ☐ Threads ☐ YT ☐ Blog ☐ Other Prompt: ☐ Freedom to write what I want _____	☐ Research ☐ Prepare entry ☐ Submit _____

Date	Primary Book Progress	Other Books & Tasks	Social Media	Contests & Promos
Sun Jul 12	Words/pages: ____	Book 2: Book 3: Book 4: Book 5:	☐ IG ☐ FB ☐ TikTok ☐ BlueSky ☐ Threads ☐ YT ☐ Blog ☐ Other _____	☐ Research ☐ Prepare entry ☐ Submit _____
Mon Jul 13	Words/pages: ____	Book 2: Book 3: Book 4: Book 5:	☐ IG ☐ FB ☐ TikTok ☐ BlueSky ☐ Threads ☐ YT ☐ Blog ☐ Other _____	☐ Research ☐ Prepare entry ☐ Submit _____
Tue Jul 14	Words/pages: ____	Book 2: Book 3: Book 4: Book 5:	☐ IG ☐ FB ☐ TikTok ☐ BlueSky ☐ Threads ☐ YT ☐ Blog ☐ Other _____	☐ Research ☐ Prepare entry ☐ Submit _____

☐ Keep notes on continuity issues to fix later

_____

_____

_____

_____

_____

_____

_____

_____

_____

_____

_____

_____

_____

_____

_____

_____

_____

Week 3 (July 15-21): Writing Week

Primary Book Weekly Task Checklist:

FINISH FIRST DRAFT:

- ☐ Complete remaining chapters and conclusion
- ☐ Daily word/page count goal: _____ words/pages per day
- ☐ Write climax and resolution
- ☐ Ensure all plot threads are addressed
- ☐ Celebrate completing first draft!

PREPARATION FOR NEXT WEEK:

- ☐ Let manuscript rest for 1-2 days if possible
- ☐ Begin cover design research and mockups
- ☐ Finalize contest submission list

Date	Primary Book Progress	Other Books & Tasks	Social Media	Contests & Promos
Wed Jul 15	Words/pages: _____	Book 2: Book 3: Book 4: Book 5:	☐ IG ☐ FB ☐ TikTok ☐ BlueSky ☐ Threads ☐ YT ☐ Blog ☐ Other Prompt: ☐ Summer writing camp/challenge	☐ Research ☐ Prepare entry ☐ Submit _____

Date	Primary Book Progress	Other Books & Tasks	Social Media	Contests & Promos
Thu Jul 16	Words/pages: _____	Book 2: Book 3: Book 4: Book 5:	☐ IG ☐ FB ☐ TikTok ☐ BlueSky ☐ Threads ☐ YT ☐ Blog ☐ Other _____	☐ Research ☐ Prepare entry ☐ Submit _____
Fri Jul 17	Words/pages: _____	Book 2: Book 3: Book 4: Book 5:	☐ IG ☐ FB ☐ TikTok ☐ BlueSky ☐ Threads ☐ YT ☐ Blog ☐ Other _____	☐ Research ☐ Prepare entry ☐ Submit _____
Sat Jul 18	Words/pages: _____	Book 2: Book 3: Book 4: Book 5:	☐ IG ☐ FB ☐ TikTok ☐ BlueSky ☐ Threads ☐ YT ☐ Blog ☐ Other _____	☐ Research ☐ Prepare entry ☐ Submit _____

Date	Primary Book Progress	Other Books & Tasks	Social Media	Contests & Promos
Sun Jul 19	Words/pages: _____	Book 2: Book 3: Book 4: Book 5:	☐ IG ☐ FB ☐ TikTok ☐ BlueSky ☐ Threads ☐ YT ☐ Blog ☐ Other Prompt: ☐ Celebrate writing independence _____	☐ Research ☐ Prepare entry ☐ Submit _____
Mon Jul 20	Words/pages: _____	Book 2: Book 3: Book 4: Book 5:	☐ IG ☐ FB ☐ TikTok ☐ BlueSky ☐ Threads ☐ YT ☐ Blog ☐ Other _____	☐ Research ☐ Prepare entry ☐ Submit _____
Tue Jul 21	Words/pages: _____	Book 2: Book 3: Book 4: Book 5:	☐ IG ☐ FB ☐ TikTok ☐ BlueSky ☐ Threads ☐ YT ☐ Blog ☐ Other _____	☐ Research ☐ Prepare entry ☐ Submit _____

Plot thread and/or cover design notes:

_____

_____

Notes:

Week 4 (July 22-31): Editing & Publishing Week

Primary Book Weekly Task Checklist:

EDITING (Days 1-3):

- ☐ Read through entire manuscript, make notes
- ☐ Fix plot holes and continuity errors
- ☐ Strengthen weak scenes and dialogue
- ☐ Cut unnecessary content, tighten prose
- ☐ Proofread for grammar, spelling, typos

COVER & FORMATTING (Days 4-5):

- ☐ Design book cover (Canva, Photoshop, or hire designer)
- ☐ Format manuscript for publication (ebook/print)
- ☐ Write book description/blurb
- ☐ Create author bio if needed

PUBLISHING & PROMOTION (Days 6-10):

- ☐ Upload to publishing platform (KDP, IngramSpark, etc.)
- ☐ Submit to contest(s): _____
- ☐ Submit to contest(s): _____
- ☐ Schedule social media announcement posts
- ☐ Update author website/portfolio
- ☐ Send to beta readers or reviewers

Date	Primary Book Progress	Other Books & Tasks	Social Media	Contests & Promos
Wed Jul 22	Words/pages: _____	Book 2: Book 3: Book 4: Book 5:	☐ IG ☐ FB ☐ TikTok ☐ BlueSky ☐ Threads ☐ YT ☐ Blog ☐ Other	☐ Research ☐ Prepare entry ☐ Submit _____

Date	Primary Book Progress	Other Books & Tasks	Social Media	Contests & Promos
Thu Jul 23	Words/pages: _____	Book 2: Book 3: Book 4: Book 5:	☐ IG ☐ FB ☐ TikTok ☐ BlueSky ☐ Threads ☐ YT ☐ Blog ☐ Other _____	☐ Research ☐ Prepare entry ☐ Submit
Fri Jul 24	Words/pages: _____	Book 2: Book 3: Book 4: Book 5:	☐ IG ☐ FB ☐ TikTok ☐ BlueSky ☐ Threads ☐ YT ☐ Blog ☐ Other _____	☐ Research ☐ Prepare entry ☐ Submit _____
Sat Jul 25	Words/pages: _____	Book 2: Book 3: Book 4: Book 5:	☐ IG ☐ FB ☐ TikTok ☐ BlueSky ☐ Threads ☐ YT ☐ Blog ☐ Other _____	☐ Research ☐ Prepare entry ☐ Submit _____

Date	Primary Book Progress	Other Books & Tasks	Social Media	Contests & Promos
Sun Jul 26	Words/pages: _____	Book 2: Book 3: Book 4: Book 5:	□ IG □ FB □ TikTok □ BlueSky □ Threads □ YT □ Blog □ Other _____	□ Research □ Prepare entry □ Submit _____
Mon Jul 27	Words/pages: _____	Book 2: Book 3: Book 4: Book 5:	□ IG □ FB □ TikTok □ BlueSky □ Threads □ YT □ Blog □ Other Prompt: □ Mid-year wins & accomplishme nts_____	□ Research □ Prepare entry □ Submit _____
Tue Jul 28	Words/pages: _____	Book 2: Book 3: Book 4: Book 5:	□ IG □ FB □ TikTok □ BlueSky □ Threads □ YT □ Blog □ Other _____	□ Research □ Prepare entry □ Submit _____

211

Date	Primary Book Progress	Other Books & Tasks	Social Media	Contests & Promos
Wed Jul 29	Words/pages: _____	Book 2: Book 3: Book 4: Book 5:	☐ IG ☐ FB ☐ TikTok ☐ BlueSky ☐ Threads ☐ YT ☐ Blog ☐ Other _____	☐ Research ☐ Prepare entry ☐ Submit _____
Thu Jul 30	Words/pages: _____	Book 2: Book 3: Book 4: Book 5:	☐ IG ☐ FB ☐ TikTok ☐ BlueSky ☐ Threads ☐ YT ☐ Blog ☐ Other _____	☐ Research ☐ Prepare entry ☐ Submit _____
Fri Jul 31	Words/pages: _____	Book 2: Book 3: Book 4: Book 5:	☐ IG ☐ FB ☐ TikTok ☐ BlueSky ☐ Threads ☐ YT ☐ Blog ☐ Other _____	☐ Research ☐ Prepare entry ☐ Submit _____

Notes:

_____

_____

_____

Designed by Jody Ortiz

July Review & Reflection

Primary Book Progress:

Status: ☐ Completed ☐ In Progress ☐ On Hold

Words/Pages Written This Month: _____

Progress on Other Books:

Book 2:
_____

Book 3:
_____

Book 4:
_____

Book 5:
_____

What worked well this month:

_____

_____

_____

_____

Challenges and solutions:

_____

_____

_____

_____

August 2026

Book to complete this month: _____

Genre: _____

Target Word/Page Count: _____

Current Stage: _____

Stage Guide:

- Planning - Outlining, research, character development

- Drafting - Active writing phase

- Revising - Content editing and restructuring

- Editing - Line editing and polishing

- Publishing Prep - Cover design, formatting, contest submissions

- Published - Promotion and marketing phase

Monthly Goals:

- Complete manuscript by day 21
- Finish editing and revisions by day 28
- Design professional cover
- Submit to at least 2 contests or promotional opportunities
- Post on social media 3x per week minimum
- _____
- _____

August 2026 - Projects Overview

Track up to 5 books in progress this month

Book	Title & Genre	Current Stage	Target Words/Pages	Month Goal
PRIMARY				
Book 2				
Book 3				
Book 4				
Book 5				

Book Color Coding Guide: Add highlighters or other shading for quick reference.

Book	Shading/Highlight Reference
PRIMARY (Book 1)	
Book 2	
Book 3	
Book 4	
Book 5	

August writing inspiration at a glance: Add these to your calendar or tape them to your computer or wherever they will inspire you.

August 1 *"To write is to carve a new path through the terrain of the imagination."* — Francesca Lia Block	**August 2** *"Writing is an act of courage."* — Natalie Goldberg
August 3 *"Do not hoard what seems good for a later place in the book; give it, give it all, give it now."* — Annie Dillard	**August 4** *"A writer is someone who has taught their mind to misbehave."* — Oscar Wilde
August 5 *"Every writer is a frustrated actor who recites their lines in the hidden auditorium of their skull."* — Rod Serling	**August 6** *"Writing is the most fun you can have by yourself."* — Terry Pratchett
August 7 *"Stories are light. Light is precious in a world so dark."* — Kate DiCamillo	**August 8** *"Writing is a leap of faith."* — Julia Cameron
August 9 *"Tears are words that need to be written."* — Paulo Coelho	**August 10** *"Write what you know. That should leave you with a lot of free time."* — Howard Nemerov

August 11 *"You must write as if you are already dead."* — Anne Enright	**August 12** *"Characters should be three-dimensional. Make them human."* — Chimamanda Ngozi Adichie
August 13 *"The truth does not change according to our ability to stomach it."* — Flannery O'Connor	**August 14** *"Write. Rewrite. When not writing or rewriting, read."* — William Faulkner
August 15 *"If you want to change the world, pick up your pen and write."* — Martin Luther	**August 16** *"I write because there is a voice within me that will not be still."* — Sylvia Plath
August 17 *"What I like in a good author is not what they say but what they whisper."* — Logan Pearsall Smith	**August 18** *"Substitute 'damn' every time you're inclined to write 'very'; your editor will delete it and the writing will be just as it should be."* — Mark Twain
August 19 *"Write freely and as rapidly as possible and throw the whole thing on paper."* — John Steinbeck	**August 20** *"Art is never finished, only abandoned."* — Leonardo da Vinci
August 21 *"If the book is true, it will find an audience that is meant to read it."* — Wally Lamb	**August 22** *"Show up, show up, show up, and after a while the muse shows up, too."* — Isabel Allende

August 23

"Every story needs a beginning, a middle, and an end. Not necessarily in that order."
— Jean-Luc Godard

August 24

"Writing is the cure for all things. There is no problem too big that writing can't solve."
— Jeanette Winterson

August 25

"Your life is your story. Write well. Edit often."
— Susan Statham

August 26

"A story is not like a road to follow... it's more like a house. You go inside and stay there for a while."
— Alice Munro

August 27

"Write the book you wish you could read."
— Adrienne Rich

August 28

"The task of the modern writer is not to make the world safe for democracy, but to make democracy safe for the world."
— J.M. Coetzee

August 29

"Writing is a bit like walking through the forest. You don't know what you'll encounter, but you keep going."
— Haruki Murakami

August 30

"Write because you love it, not because you want to be loved."
— Unknown

August 31

"The work never matches the dream of perfection the artist has to start with."
— William Faulkner

August Social Media Planning

Monthly Social Media Goals & Tracking

Platform	Goal Posts	Completed	Content Ideas / Notes
Instagram	____	____	
Facebook	____	____	
TikTok	____	____	
BlueSky	____	____	
Threads	____	____	
LinkedIn	____	____	
YouTube/Shorts	____	____	
Pinterest	____	____	
Goodreads	____	____	
BookBub	____	____	
Author Website/Blog	____	____	

Weekly Social Media Content Calendar:

- Week 1: Behind-the-scenes character/plot development
- Week 2: Writing progress updates, word count milestones
- Week 3: First draft completion celebration, cover reveals

221

- **Week 4:** Book announcement, pre-order/launch details, contest entries

August Contest & Promotional Opportunities

Track submissions and deadlines

Contest/Opportunity	Deadline	Status	Entry Fee	Notes/Requirements
		☐ Plan ☐ Submit ☐ Done	$_____	
		☐ Plan ☐ Submit ☐ Done	$_____	
		☐ Plan ☐ Submit ☐ Done	$_____	
		☐ Plan ☐ Submit ☐ Done	$_____	
		☐ Plan ☐ Submit ☐ Done	$_____	
		☐ Plan ☐ Submit ☐ Done	$_____	
		☐ Plan ☐ Submit ☐ Done	$_____	
		☐ Plan ☐ Submit ☐ Done	$_____	
		☐ Plan ☐ Submit ☐ Done	$_____	
		☐ Plan ☐ Submit ☐ Done	$_____	

Promotional Opportunities Checklist:

- ☐ Book review blogs and websites
- ☐ BookTok/Bookstagram influencer outreach
- ☐ Goodreads giveaway or promotion
- ☐ BookBub featured deal submission
- ☐ Amazon/KDP advertising campaign
- ☐ Author newsletter announcement
- ☐ Podcast interview pitches
- ☐ Local bookstore/library events
- ☐ Cross-promotion with other authors
- ☐ Book club outreach

Stage Guide:

- Planning - Outlining, research, character development
- Drafting - Active writing phase
- Revising - Content editing and restructuring
- Editing - Line editing and polishing
- Publishing Prep - Cover design, formatting, contest submissions
- Published - Promotion and marketing phase

Week 1 (August 1-7): Writing Week

Primary Book Weekly Task Checklist:

PLANNING & SETUP (Days 1-3):

- ☐ Develop main characters (names, traits, motivations, arcs)
- ☐ Create basic plot outline or beat sheet
- ☐ Define key settings and world-building elements
- ☐ Research any necessary details for authenticity

WRITING BEGINS (Days 4-7):

- ☐ Write opening chapters (aim for 25% of target word count)
- ☐ Daily word/page count goal: _____ words/pages per day
- ☐ Establish narrative voice and tone
- ☐ Research 2-3 potential contests to enter

Date	Primary Book Progress	Other Books & Tasks	Social Media	Contests & Promos
Sat Aug 1	Words/pages: _____	Book 2: Book 3: Book 4: Book 5:	☐ IG ☐ FB ☐ TikTok ☐ BlueSky ☐ Threads ☐ YT ☐ Blog ☐ Other	☐ Research ☐ Prepare entry ☐ Submit _____

Date	Primary Book Progress	Other Books & Tasks	Social Media	Contests & Promos
Sun Aug 2	Words/pages: _____	Book 2: Book 3: Book 4: Book 5:	☐ IG ☐ FB ☐ TikTok ☐ BlueSky ☐ Threads ☐ YT ☐ Blog ☐ Other _____	☐ Research ☐ Prepare entry ☐ Submit _____
Mon Aug 3	Words/pages: _____	Book 2: Book 3: Book 4: Book 5:	☐ IG ☐ FB ☐ TikTok ☐ BlueSky ☐ Threads ☐ YT ☐ Blog ☐ Other Prompt: ☐ Back-to-school nostalgia & books _____	☐ Research ☐ Prepare entry ☐ Submit _____
Tue Aug 4	Words/pages: _____	Book 2: Book 3: Book 4: Book 5:	☐ IG ☐ FB ☐ TikTok ☐ BlueSky ☐ Threads ☐ YT ☐ Blog ☐ Other _____	☐ Research ☐ Prepare entry ☐ Submit _____

Date	Primary Book Progress	Other Books & Tasks	Social Media	Contests & Promos
Wed Aug 5	Words/pages: _____	Book 2: Book 3: Book 4: Book 5:	☐ IG ☐ FB ☐ TikTok ☐ BlueSky ☐ Threads ☐ YT ☐ Blog ☐ Other _____	☐ Research ☐ Prepare entry ☐ Submit
Thu Aug 6	Words/pages: _____	Book 2: Book 3: Book 4: Book 5:	☐ IG ☐ FB ☐ TikTok ☐ BlueSky ☐ Threads ☐ YT ☐ Blog ☐ Other Prompt: ☐ Writing tools & supplies haul	☐ Research ☐ Prepare entry ☐ Submit _____
Fri Aug 7	Words/pages: _____	Book 2: Book 3: Book 4: Book 5:	☐ IG ☐ FB ☐ TikTok ☐ BlueSky ☐ Threads ☐ YT ☐ Blog ☐ Other _____	☐ Research ☐ Prepare entry ☐ Submit _____

Notes:

Week 2 (August 8-14): Writing Week

Primary Book Weekly Task Checklist:

INTENSIVE WRITING WEEK:

- ☐ Write middle section chapters (aim for 40-50% of total manuscript)
- ☐ Daily word/page count goal: _____ words/pages per day
- ☐ Build tension and develop character relationships
- ☐ Keep notes on continuity issues to fix later
- ☐ Don't edit yet - focus on getting words on the page

MARKETING PREP:

- ☐ Draft social media posts about your writing progress
- ☐ Start thinking about cover concepts

Date	Primary Book Progress	Other Books & Tasks	Social Media	Contests & Promos
Sat Aug 8	Words/pages: _____	Book 2: Book 3: Book 4: Book 5:	☐ IG ☐ FB ☐ TikTok ☐ BlueSky ☐ Threads ☐ YT ☐ Blog ☐ Other	☐ Research ☐ Prepare entry ☐ Submit

Date	Primary Book Progress	Other Books & Tasks	Social Media	Contests & Promos
Sun Aug 9	Words/pages: _____	Book 2: Book 3: Book 4: Book 5:	☐ IG ☐ FB ☐ TikTok ☐ BlueSky ☐ Threads ☐ YT ☐ Blog ☐ Other Prompt: ☐ National Book Lovers Day _____	☐ Research ☐ Prepare entry ☐ Submit _____
Mon Aug 10	Words/pages: _____	Book 2: Book 3: Book 4: Book 5:	☐ IG ☐ FB ☐ TikTok ☐ BlueSky ☐ Threads ☐ YT ☐ Blog ☐ Other _____	☐ Research ☐ Prepare entry ☐ Submit _____
Tue Aug 11	Words/pages: _____	Book 2: Book 3: Book 4: Book 5:	☐ IG ☐ FB ☐ TikTok ☐ BlueSky ☐ Threads ☐ YT ☐ Blog ☐ Other _____	☐ Research ☐ Prepare entry ☐ Submit _____

Date	Primary Book Progress	Other Books & Tasks	Social Media	Contests & Promos
Wed Aug 12	Words/pages: _____	Book 2: Book 3: Book 4: Book 5:	☐ IG ☐ FB ☐ TikTok ☐ BlueSky ☐ Threads ☐ YT ☐ Blog ☐ Other	☐ Research ☐ Prepare entry ☐ Submit
Thu Aug 13	Words/pages: _____	Book 2: Book 3: Book 4: Book 5:	☐ IG ☐ FB ☐ TikTok ☐ BlueSky ☐ Threads ☐ YT ☐ Blog ☐ Other Prompt: ☐ What I'm learning as a writer	☐ Research ☐ Prepare entry ☐ Submit
Fri Aug 14	Words/pages: _____	Book 2: Book 3: Book 4: Book 5:	☐ IG ☐ FB ☐ TikTok ☐ BlueSky ☐ Threads ☐ YT ☐ Blog ☐ Other	☐ Research ☐ Prepare entry ☐ Submit

☐ Keep notes on continuity issues to fix later

_____

_____

_____

_____

_____

_____

_____

_____

_____

_____

_____

_____

_____

_____

_____

_____

_____

_____

Week 3 (August 15-21): Writing Week

Primary Book Weekly Task Checklist:

FINISH FIRST DRAFT:

- ☐ Complete remaining chapters and conclusion
- ☐ Daily word/page count goal: _____ words/pages per day
- ☐ Write climax and resolution
- ☐ Ensure all plot threads are addressed
- ☐ Celebrate completing first draft!

PREPARATION FOR NEXT WEEK:

- ☐ Let manuscript rest for 1-2 days if possible
- ☐ Begin cover design research and mockups
- ☐ Finalize contest submission list

Date	Primary Book Progress	Other Books & Tasks	Social Media	Contests & Promos
Sat Aug 15	Words/pages: _____	Book 2: Book 3: Book 4: Book 5:	☐ IG ☐ FB ☐ TikTok ☐ BlueSky ☐ Threads ☐ YT ☐ Blog ☐ Other	☐ Research ☐ Prepare entry ☐ Submit _____

Date	Primary Book Progress	Other Books & Tasks	Social Media	Contests & Promos
Sun Aug 16	Words/pages: _____	Book 2: Book 3: Book 4: Book 5:	☐ IG ☐ FB ☐ TikTok ☐ BlueSky ☐ Threads ☐ YT ☐ Blog ☐ Other _____	☐ Research ☐ Prepare entry ☐ Submit _____
Mon Aug 17	Words/pages: _____	Book 2: Book 3: Book 4: Book 5:	☐ IG ☐ FB ☐ TikTok ☐ BlueSky ☐ Threads ☐ YT ☐ Blog ☐ Other Prompt: ☐ Research rabbit holes you've fallen into	☐ Research ☐ Prepare entry ☐ Submit _____
Tue Aug 18	Words/pages: _____	Book 2: Book 3: Book 4: Book 5:	☐ IG ☐ FB ☐ TikTok ☐ BlueSky ☐ Threads ☐ YT ☐ Blog ☐ Other _____	☐ Research ☐ Prepare entry ☐ Submit _____

233

Date	Primary Book Progress	Other Books & Tasks	Social Media	Contests & Promos
Wed Aug 19	Words/pages: _____	Book 2: Book 3: Book 4: Book 5:	☐ IG ☐ FB ☐ TikTok ☐ BlueSky ☐ Threads ☐ YT ☐ Blog ☐ Other _____	☐ Research ☐ Prepare entry ☐ Submit _____
Thu Aug 20	Words/pages: _____	Book 2: Book 3: Book 4: Book 5:	☐ IG ☐ FB ☐ TikTok ☐ BlueSky ☐ Threads ☐ YT ☐ Blog ☐ Other Prompt: ☐ Prep for fall release season _____	☐ Research ☐ Prepare entry ☐ Submit _____
Fri Aug 21	Words/pages: _____	Book 2: Book 3: Book 4: Book 5:	☐ IG ☐ FB ☐ TikTok ☐ BlueSky ☐ Threads ☐ YT ☐ Blog ☐ Other _____	☐ Research ☐ Prepare entry ☐ Submit _____

Plot thread and/or cover design notes:

_____

_____

_____

Notes:

Week 4 (August 22-31): Editing & Publishing Week

Primary Book Weekly Task Checklist:

EDITING (Days 1-3):

- ☐ Read through entire manuscript, make notes
- ☐ Fix plot holes and continuity errors
- ☐ Strengthen weak scenes and dialogue
- ☐ Cut unnecessary content, tighten prose
- ☐ Proofread for grammar, spelling, typos

COVER & FORMATTING (Days 4-5):

- ☐ Design book cover (Canva, Photoshop, or hire designer)
- ☐ Format manuscript for publication (ebook/print)
- ☐ Write book description/blurb
- ☐ Create author bio if needed

PUBLISHING & PROMOTION (Days 6-10):

- ☐ Upload to publishing platform (KDP, IngramSpark, etc.)
- ☐ Submit to contest(s): _____
- ☐ Submit to contest(s): _____
- ☐ Schedule social media announcement posts
- ☐ Update author website/portfolio
- ☐ Send to beta readers or reviewers

Date	Primary Book Progress	Other Books & Tasks	Social Media	Contests & Promos
Sat Aug 22	Words/pages: _____	Book 2: Book 3: Book 4: Book 5:	☐ IG ☐ FB ☐ TikTok ☐ BlueSky ☐ Threads ☐ YT ☐ Blog ☐ Other	☐ Research ☐ Prepare entry ☐ Submit _____

Date	Primary Book Progress	Other Books & Tasks	Social Media	Contests & Promos
Sun Aug 23	Words/pages: _____	Book 2: Book 3: Book 4: Book 5:	☐ IG ☐ FB ☐ TikTok ☐ BlueSky ☐ Threads ☐ YT ☐ Blog ☐ Other _____	☐ Research ☐ Prepare entry ☐ Submit _____
Mon Aug 24	Words/pages: _____	Book 2: Book 3: Book 4: Book 5:	☐ IG ☐ FB ☐ TikTok ☐ BlueSky ☐ Threads ☐ YT ☐ Blog ☐ Other _____	☐ Research ☐ Prepare entry ☐ Submit _____
Tue Aug 25	Words/pages: _____	Book 2: Book 3: Book 4: Book 5:	☐ IG ☐ FB ☐ TikTok ☐ BlueSky ☐ Threads ☐ YT ☐ Blog ☐ Other _____	☐ Research ☐ Prepare entry ☐ Submit _____

Date	Primary Book Progress	Other Books & Tasks	Social Media	Contests & Promos
Wed Aug 26	Words/pages: _____	Book 2: Book 3: Book 4: Book 5:	☐ IG ☐ FB ☐ TikTok ☐ BlueSky ☐ Threads ☐ YT ☐ Blog ☐ Other _____	☐ Research ☐ Prepare entry ☐ Submit _____
Thu Aug 27	Words/pages: _____	Book 2: Book 3: Book 4: Book 5:	☐ IG ☐ FB ☐ TikTok ☐ BlueSky ☐ Threads ☐ YT ☐ Blog ☐ Other _____	☐ Research ☐ Prepare entry ☐ Submit _____
Fri Aug 28	Words/pages: _____	Book 2: Book 3: Book 4: Book 5:	☐ IG ☐ FB ☐ TikTok ☐ BlueSky ☐ Threads ☐ YT ☐ Blog ☐ Other _____	☐ Research ☐ Prepare entry ☐ Submit _____

Date	Primary Book Progress	Other Books & Tasks	Social Media	Contests & Promos
Sat Aug 29	Words/pages: _____	Book 2: Book 3: Book 4: Book 5:	☐ IG ☐ FB ☐ TikTok ☐ BlueSky ☐ Threads ☐ YT ☐ Blog ☐ Other _____	☐ Research ☐ Prepare entry ☐ Submit _____
Sun Aug 30	Words/pages: _____	Book 2: Book 3: Book 4: Book 5:	☐ IG ☐ FB ☐ TikTok ☐ BlueSky ☐ Threads ☐ YT ☐ Blog ☐ Other _____	☐ Research ☐ Prepare entry ☐ Submit _____
Mon Aug 31	Words/pages: _____	Book 2: Book 3: Book 4: Book 5:	☐ IG ☐ FB ☐ TikTok ☐ BlueSky ☐ Threads ☐ YT ☐ Blog ☐ Other _____	☐ Research ☐ Prepare entry ☐ Submit _____

Notes:

_____

_____

_____

Designed by Jody Ortiz

August Review & Reflection

Primary Book Progress:

Status: ☐ Completed   ☐ In Progress   ☐ On Hold

Words/Pages Written This Month: _____

Progress on Other Books:

Book 2:

_____

Book 3:

_____

Book 4:

_____

Book 5:

_____

What worked well this month:

_____

_____

_____

_____

Challenges and solutions:

_____

_____

_____

_____

September 2026

Book to complete this month: _____

Genre: _____

Target Word/Page Count: _____

Current Stage: _____

Stage Guide:

- Planning - Outlining, research, character development

- Drafting - Active writing phase

- Revising - Content editing and restructuring

- Editing - Line editing and polishing

- Publishing Prep - Cover design, formatting, contest submissions

- Published - Promotion and marketing phase

Monthly Goals:

- Complete manuscript by day 21
- Finish editing and revisions by day 28
- Design professional cover
- Submit to at least 2 contests or promotional opportunities
- Post on social media 3x per week minimum
- _____
- _____

September 2026 - Projects Overview

Track up to 5 books in progress this month

Book	Title & Genre	Current Stage	Target Words/Pages	Month Goal
PRIMARY				
Book 2				
Book 3				
Book 4				
Book 5				

Book Color Coding Guide: Add highlighters or other shading for quick reference.

Book	Shading/Highlight Reference
PRIMARY (Book 1)	
Book 2	
Book 3	
Book 4	
Book 5	

September writing inspiration at a glance: Add these to your calendar or tape them to your computer or wherever they will inspire you.

September 1	September 2
"Write a short story every week. It's not possible to write 52 bad short stories in a row." — Ray Bradbury	*"My task is to make you hear, to make you feel, and above all, to make you see."* — Joseph Conrad
September 3	**September 4**
"We have to create culture, don't watch TV, don't read magazines, don't even listen to NPR. Create your own roadshow." — Terence McKenna	*"Writing is its own reward. The day I discover it isn't, I'll stop."* — Larry Niven
September 5	**September 6**
"You can fix anything but a blank page." — Nora Roberts	*"The best writing is rewriting."* — E.B. White
September 7	**September 8**
"If you want to write, write it. That's the first rule." — Robert Parker	*"If you have any young friends who aspire to become writers, the second greatest favor you can do them is to present them with copies of The Elements of Style."* — E.B. White
September 9	**September 10**
"Writing requires a great deal of patience and endurance." — Mary Oliver	*"The only kind of writing is rewriting."* — Ernest Hemingway

September 11	**September 12**
"Fiction is the truth inside the lie." — Stephen King	*"Half my life is an act of revision."* — John Irving

September 13	**September 14**
"In writing, you must kill all your darlings." — William Faulkner	*"A writer never has a vacation. For a writer, life consists of either writing or thinking about writing."* — Eugène Ionesco

September 15	**September 16**
"When writing the story of your life, don't let anyone else hold the pen." — Harley Davidson	*"Action is character."* — F. Scott Fitzgerald

September 17	**September 18**
"I try to leave out the parts that people skip." — Elmore Leonard	*"The writing life is essentially one of solitary confinement—if you can't deal with this, you needn't apply."* — Will Self

September 19	**September 20**
"A writer is a person for whom writing is more difficult than it is for other people." — Thomas Mann	*"Consistency is the last refuge of the unimaginative."* — Oscar Wilde

September 21	**September 22**
"Write quickly and you will never write well; write well and you will soon write quickly." — Quintilian	*"If you hear a voice within you say 'you cannot paint,' then by all means paint, and that voice will be silenced."* — Vincent van Gogh

September 23

"First drafts are for learning what your novel is about."

— Bernard Malamud

September 24

"The secret of being a bore is to tell everything."

— Voltaire

September 25

"Don't be afraid to give up the good to go for the great."

— John D. Rockefeller

September 26

"The faster I write the better my output. If I'm going slow, I'm in trouble."

— Raymond Chandler

September 27

"I would advise anyone who aspires to a writing career that before developing their talent they would be wise to develop a thick hide."

— Harper Lee

September 28

"Writing a book is an adventure. To begin with it is a toy and an amusement. Then it becomes a mistress, then it becomes a master, then it becomes a tyrant."

— Winston Churchill

September 29

"If writing seems hard, it's because it is hard."

— William Zinsser

September 30

"I don't care if a reader hates one of my stories, just as long as they finish the book."

— Roald Dahl

September Social Media Planning

Monthly Social Media Goals & Tracking

Platform	Goal Posts	Completed	Content Ideas / Notes
Instagram	____	____	
Facebook	____	____	
TikTok	____	____	
BlueSky	____	____	
Threads	____	____	
LinkedIn	____	____	
YouTube/Shorts	____	____	
Pinterest	____	____	
Goodreads	____	____	
BookBub	____	____	
Author Website/Blog	____	____	

Weekly Social Media Content Calendar:

- Week 1: Behind-the-scenes character/plot development
- Week 2: Writing progress updates, word count milestones
- Week 3: First draft completion celebration, cover reveals

248

- Week 4: Book announcement, pre-order/launch details, contest entries

September Contest & Promotional Opportunities

Track submissions and deadlines

Contest/Opportunity	Deadline	Status	Entry Fee	Notes/Requirements
		☐ Plan ☐ Submit ☐ Done	$_____	
		☐ Plan ☐ Submit ☐ Done	$_____	
		☐ Plan ☐ Submit ☐ Done	$_____	
		☐ Plan ☐ Submit ☐ Done	$_____	
		☐ Plan ☐ Submit ☐ Done	$_____	
		☐ Plan ☐ Submit ☐ Done	$_____	
		☐ Plan ☐ Submit ☐ Done	$_____	
		☐ Plan ☐ Submit ☐ Done	$_____	
		☐ Plan ☐ Submit ☐ Done	$_____	
		☐ Plan ☐ Submit ☐ Done	$_____	

Promotional Opportunities Checklist:

- ☐ Book review blogs and websites
- ☐ BookTok/Bookstagram influencer outreach
- ☐ Goodreads giveaway or promotion
- ☐ BookBub featured deal submission
- ☐ Amazon/KDP advertising campaign
- ☐ Author newsletter announcement
- ☐ Podcast interview pitches
- ☐ Local bookstore/library events
- ☐ Cross-promotion with other authors
- ☐ Book club outreach

Stage Guide:

- Planning - Outlining, research, character development
- Drafting - Active writing phase
- Revising - Content editing and restructuring
- Editing - Line editing and polishing
- Publishing Prep - Cover design, formatting, contest submissions
- Published - Promotion and marketing phase

Week 1 (September 1-7): Writing Week

Primary Book Weekly Task Checklist:

PLANNING & SETUP (Days 1-3):

- ☐ Develop main characters (names, traits, motivations, arcs)
- ☐ Create basic plot outline or beat sheet
- ☐ Define key settings and world-building elements
- ☐ Research any necessary details for authenticity

WRITING BEGINS (Days 4-7):

- ☐ Write opening chapters (aim for 25% of target word count)
- ☐ Daily word/page count goal: _____ words/pages per day
- ☐ Establish narrative voice and tone
- ☐ Research 2-3 potential contests to enter

Date	Primary Book Progress	Other Books & Tasks	Social Media	Contests & Promos
Tue Sep 1	Words/pages: _____	Book 2: Book 3: Book 4: Book 5:	☐ IG ☐ FB ☐ TikTok ☐ BlueSky ☐ Threads ☐ YT ☐ Blog ☐ Other Prompt: ☐ Autumn-themed book recommendations _____	☐ Research ☐ Prepare entry ☐ Submit _____

Date	Primary Book Progress	Other Books & Tasks	Social Media	Contests & Promos
Wed Sep 2	Words/pages: _____	Book 2: Book 3: Book 4: Book 5:	☐ IG ☐ FB ☐ TikTok ☐ BlueSky ☐ Threads ☐ YT ☐ Blog ☐ Other _____	☐ Research ☐ Prepare entry ☐ Submit _____
Thu Sep 3	Words/pages: _____	Book 2: Book 3: Book 4: Book 5:	☐ IG ☐ FB ☐ TikTok ☐ BlueSky ☐ Threads ☐ YT ☐ Blog ☐ Other _____	☐ Research ☐ Prepare entry ☐ Submit _____
Fri Sep 4	Words/pages: _____	Book 2: Book 3: Book 4: Book 5:	☐ IG ☐ FB ☐ TikTok ☐ BlueSky ☐ Threads ☐ YT ☐ Blog ☐ Other _____	☐ Research ☐ Prepare entry ☐ Submit _____

Date	Primary Book Progress	Other Books & Tasks	Social Media	Contests & Promos
Sat Sep 5	Words/pages: _____	Book 2: Book 3: Book 4: Book 5:	☐ IG ☐ FB ☐ TikTok ☐ BlueSky ☐ Threads ☐ YT ☐ Blog ☐ Other _____	☐ Research ☐ Prepare entry ☐ Submit _____
Sun Sep 6	Words/pages: _____	Book 2: Book 3: Book 4: Book 5:	☐ IG ☐ FB ☐ TikTok ☐ BlueSky ☐ Threads ☐ YT ☐ Blog ☐ Other _____	☐ Research ☐ Prepare entry ☐ Submit _____
Mon Sep 7	Words/pages: _____	Book 2: Book 3: Book 4: Book 5:	☐ IG ☐ FB ☐ TikTok ☐ BlueSky ☐ Threads ☐ YT ☐ Blog ☐ Other _____	☐ Research ☐ Prepare entry ☐ Submit _____

Notes:

_____
_____
_____

Week 2 (September 8-14): Writing Week

Primary Book Weekly Task Checklist:

INTENSIVE WRITING WEEK:

- ☐ Write middle section chapters (aim for 40-50% of total manuscript)
- ☐ Daily word/page count goal: _____ words/pages per day
- ☐ Build tension and develop character relationships
- ☐ Keep notes on continuity issues to fix later
- ☐ Don't edit yet - focus on getting words on the page

MARKETING PREP:

- ☐ Draft social media posts about your writing progress
- ☐ Start thinking about cover concepts

Date	Primary Book Progress	Other Books & Tasks	Social Media	Contests & Promos
Tue Sep 8	Words/pages: _____	Book 2: Book 3: Book 4: Book 5:	☐ IG ☐ FB ☐ TikTok ☐ BlueSky ☐ Threads ☐ YT ☐ Blog ☐ Other	☐ Research ☐ Prepare entry ☐ Submit

255

Date	Primary Book Progress	Other Books & Tasks	Social Media	Contests & Promos
Wed Sep 9	Words/pages: _____	Book 2: Book 3: Book 4: Book 5:	□ IG □ FB □ TikTok □ BlueSky □ Threads □ YT □ Blog □ Other Prompt: □ Cozy writing season begins _____	□ Research □ Prepare entry □ Submit _____
Thu Sep 10	Words/pages: _____	Book 2: Book 3: Book 4: Book 5:	□ IG □ FB □ TikTok □ BlueSky □ Threads □ YT □ Blog □ Other _____	□ Research □ Prepare entry □ Submit _____
Fri Sep 11	Words/pages: _____	Book 2: Book 3: Book 4: Book 5:	□ IG □ FB □ TikTok □ BlueSky □ Threads □ YT □ Blog □ Other _____	□ Research □ Prepare entry □ Submit _____

Date	Primary Book Progress	Other Books & Tasks	Social Media	Contests & Promos
Sat Sep 12	Words/pages: _____	Book 2: Book 3: Book 4: Book 5:	☐ IG ☐ FB ☐ TikTok ☐ BlueSky ☐ Threads ☐ YT ☐ Blog ☐ Other _____	☐ Research ☐ Prepare cntry ☐ Submit _____
Sun Sep 13	Words/pages: _____	Book 2: Book 3: Book 4: Book 5:	☐ IG ☐ FB ☐ TikTok ☐ BlueSky ☐ Threads ☐ YT ☐ Blog ☐ Other _____	☐ Research ☐ Prepare entry ☐ Submit _____
Mon Sep 14	Words/pages: _____	Book 2: Book 3: Book 4: Book 5:	☐ IG ☐ FB ☐ TikTok ☐ BlueSky ☐ Threads ☐ YT ☐ Blog ☐ Other Prompt: ☐ Favorite fall writing rituals _____	☐ Research ☐ Prepare entry ☐ Submit _____

☐ Keep notes on continuity issues to fix later

_____

_____

_____

_____

_____

_____

_____

_____

_____

_____

_____

_____

_____

_____

_____

_____

WRITE MORE FUCKING BOOKS!

Week 3 (September 15-21): Writing Week

Primary Book Weekly Task Checklist:

FINISH FIRST DRAFT:

- ☐ Complete remaining chapters and conclusion
- ☐ Daily word/page count goal: _____ words/pages per day
- ☐ Write climax and resolution
- ☐ Ensure all plot threads are addressed
- ☐ Celebrate completing first draft!

PREPARATION FOR NEXT WEEK:

- ☐ Let manuscript rest for 1-2 days if possible
- ☐ Begin cover design research and mockups
- ☐ Finalize contest submission list

Date	Primary Book Progress	Other Books & Tasks	Social Media	Contests & Promos
Tue Sep 15	Words/pages: _____	Book 2: Book 3: Book 4: Book 5:	☐ IG ☐ FB ☐ TikTok ☐ BlueSky ☐ Threads ☐ YT ☐ Blog ☐ Other Prompt: ☐ Back catalog promotion	☐ Research ☐ Prepare entry ☐ Submit _____

Date	Primary Book Progress	Other Books & Tasks	Social Media	Contests & Promos
Wed Sep 16	Words/pages: _____	Book 2: Book 3: Book 4: Book 5:	☐ IG ☐ FB ☐ TikTok ☐ BlueSky ☐ Threads ☐ YT ☐ Blog ☐ Other _____	☐ Research ☐ Prepare entry ☐ Submit _____
Thu Sep 17	Words/pages: _____	Book 2: Book 3: Book 4: Book 5:	☐ IG ☐ FB ☐ TikTok ☐ BlueSky ☐ Threads ☐ YT ☐ Blog ☐ Other _____	☐ Research ☐ Prepare entry ☐ Submit _____
Fri Sep 18	Words/pages: _____	Book 2: Book 3: Book 4: Book 5:	☐ IG ☐ FB ☐ TikTok ☐ BlueSky ☐ Threads ☐ YT ☐ Blog ☐ Other _____	☐ Research ☐ Prepare entry ☐ Submit _____

Date	Primary Book Progress	Other Books & Tasks	Social Media	Contests & Promos
Sat Sep 19	Words/pages: _____	Book 2: Book 3: Book 4: Book 5:	☐ IG ☐ FB ☐ TikTok ☐ BlueSky ☐ Threads ☐ YT ☐ Blog ☐ Other Prompt: ☐ Spooky story teaser (Halloween prep)	☐ Research ☐ Prepare entry ☐ Submit _____
Sun Sep 20	Words/pages: _____	Book 2: Book 3: Book 4: Book 5:	☐ IG ☐ FB ☐ TikTok ☐ BlueSky ☐ Threads ☐ YT ☐ Blog ☐ Other	☐ Research ☐ Prepare entry ☐ Submit _____
Mon Sep 21	Words/pages: _____	Book 2: Book 3: Book 4: Book 5:	☐ IG ☐ FB ☐ TikTok ☐ BlueSky ☐ Threads ☐ YT ☐ Blog ☐ Other	☐ Research ☐ Prepare entry ☐ Submit _____

Plot thread and/or cover design notes:

_____
_____
_____
_____
_____
_____
_____
_____
_____
_____
_____
_____

Notes:

_____
_____
_____
_____
_____
_____
_____
_____
_____
_____
_____
_____
_____
_____
_____
_____
_____
_____
_____
_____
_____

Week 4 (September 22-30): Editing & Publishing Week

Primary Book Weekly Task Checklist:

EDITING (Days 1-3):

- ☐ Read through entire manuscript, make notes
- ☐ Fix plot holes and continuity errors
- ☐ Strengthen weak scenes and dialogue
- ☐ Cut unnecessary content, tighten prose
- ☐ Proofread for grammar, spelling, typos

COVER & FORMATTING (Days 4-5):

- ☐ Design book cover (Canva, Photoshop, or hire designer)
- ☐ Format manuscript for publication (ebook/print)
- ☐ Write book description/blurb
- ☐ Create author bio if needed

PUBLISHING & PROMOTION (Days 6-9):

- ☐ Upload to publishing platform (KDP, IngramSpark, etc.)
- ☐ Submit to contest(s): _____
- ☐ Submit to contest(s): _____
- ☐ Schedule social media announcement posts
- ☐ Update author website/portfolio
- ☐ Send to beta readers or reviewers

Date	Primary Book Progress	Other Books & Tasks	Social Media	Contests & Promos
Tue Sep 22	Words/pages: _____	Book 2: Book 3: Book 4: Book 5:	☐ IG ☐ FB ☐ TikTok ☐ BlueSky ☐ Threads ☐ YT ☐ Blog ☐ Other _____	☐ Research ☐ Prepare entry ☐ Submit
Wed Sep 23	Words/pages: _____	Book 2: Book 3: Book 4: Book 5:	☐ IG ☐ FB ☐ TikTok ☐ BlueSky ☐ Threads ☐ YT ☐ Blog ☐ Other _____	☐ Research ☐ Prepare entry ☐ Submit _____
Thu Sep 24	Words/pages: _____	Book 2: Book 3: Book 4: Book 5:	☐ IG ☐ FB ☐ TikTok ☐ BlueSky ☐ Threads ☐ YT ☐ Blog ☐ Other _____	☐ Research ☐ Prepare entry ☐ Submit _____

Date	Primary Book Progress	Other Books & Tasks	Social Media	Contests & Promos
Fri Sep 25	Words/pages: _____	Book 2: Book 3: Book 4: Book 5:	☐ IG ☐ FB ☐ TikTok ☐ BlueSky ☐ Threads ☐ YT ☐ Blog ☐ Other _____	☐ Research ☐ Prepare entry ☐ Submit _____
Sat Sep 26	Words/pages: _____	Book 2: Book 3: Book 4: Book 5:	☐ IG ☐ FB ☐ TikTok ☐ BlueSky ☐ Threads ☐ YT ☐ Blog ☐ Other _____	☐ Research ☐ Prepare entry ☐ Submit _____
Sun Sep 27	Words/pages: _____	Book 2: Book 3: Book 4: Book 5:	☐ IG ☐ FB ☐ TikTok ☐ BlueSky ☐ Threads ☐ YT ☐ Blog ☐ Other _____	☐ Research ☐ Prepare entry ☐ Submit _____

Date	Primary Book Progress	Other Books & Tasks	Social Media	Contests & Promos
Mon Sep 28	Words/pages: _____	Book 2: Book 3: Book 4: Book 5:	☐ IG ☐ FB ☐ TikTok ☐ BlueSky ☐ Threads ☐ YT ☐ Blog ☐ Other _____	☐ Research ☐ Prepare entry ☐ Submit _____
Tue Sep 29	Words/pages: _____	Book 2: Book 3: Book 4: Book 5:	☐ IG ☐ FB ☐ TikTok ☐ BlueSky ☐ Threads ☐ YT ☐ Blog ☐ Other Prompt: ☐ Q3 recap & Q4 goals _____	☐ Research ☐ Prepare entry ☐ Submit _____
Wed Sep 30	Words/pages: _____	Book 2: Book 3: Book 4: Book 5:	☐ IG ☐ FB ☐ TikTok ☐ BlueSky ☐ Threads ☐ YT ☐ Blog ☐ Other _____	☐ Research ☐ Prepare entry ☐ Submit _____

Notes:

_____

_____

_____

Designed by Jody Ortiz

September Review & Reflection

Primary Book Progress:

Status: ☐ Completed ☐ In Progress ☐ On Hold

Words/Pages Written This Month: _____

Progress on Other Books:

Book 2:

_____

Book 3:

_____

Book 4:

_____

Book 5:

_____

What worked well this month:

_____

_____

_____

_____

Challenges and solutions:

_____

_____

_____

_____

Q3 2026

July - September

JULY	AUGUST	SEPTEMBER
BOOK 1	BOOK 1	BOOK 1
Title:	Title:	Title:
_____	_____	_____
Genre:	Genre:	Genre:
_____	_____	_____
Status:	Status:	Status:
_____	_____	_____
BOOK 2	BOOK 2	BOOK 2
Title:	Title:	Title:
_____	_____	_____
Genre:	Genre:	Genre:
_____	_____	_____
Status:	Status:	Status:
_____	_____	_____
BOOK 3	BOOK 3	BOOK 3
Title:	Title:	Title:
_____	_____	_____
Genre:	Genre:	Genre:
_____	_____	_____
Status:	Status:	Status:
_____	_____	_____

Q3 KEY DEADLINES & MILESTONES

_____

_____

_____

_____

_____

_____

_____

_____

_____

_____

Q3 REFLECTIONS & WINS

_____

_____

_____

_____

_____

_____

October 2026

Book to complete this month: _____

Genre: _____

Target Word/Page Count: _____

Current Stage: _____

Stage Guide:

- Planning - Outlining, research, character development

- Drafting - Active writing phase

- Revising - Content editing and restructuring

- Editing - Line editing and polishing

- Publishing Prep - Cover design, formatting, contest submissions

- Published - Promotion and marketing phase

Monthly Goals:

- Complete manuscript by day 21
- Finish editing and revisions by day 28
- Design professional cover
- Submit to at least 2 contests or promotional opportunities
- Post on social media 3x per week minimum
- _____
- _____

October 2026 - Projects Overview

Track up to 5 books in progress this month

Book	Title & Genre	Current Stage	Target Words/Pages	Month Goal
PRIMARY				
Book 2				
Book 3				
Book 4				
Book 5				

Book Color Coding Guide: Add highlighters or other shading for quick reference.

Book	Shading/Highlight Reference
PRIMARY (Book 1)	
Book 2	
Book 3	
Book 4	
Book 5	

October writing inspiration at a glance: Add these to your calendar or tape them to your computer or wherever they will inspire you.

October 1	October 2
"The only thing I was fit for was to be a writer, and this notion rested solely on my suspicion that I would never be fit for real work." — Russell Baker	*"Writing is my way of making sense of the world."* — Alison Bechdel
October 3	**October 4**
"Words have meaning and names have power." — Unknown	*"Writers are not just observers; we are participants in life."* — Chimamanda Ngozi Adichie
October 5	**October 6**
"Rejection is part of writing. If you're not being rejected, you're not trying hard enough." — Unknown	*"I am irritated by my own writing. I am like a violinist whose ear is true, but whose fingers refuse to reproduce precisely the sound heard within."* — Gustave Flaubert
October 7	**October 8**
"I write to understand as much as to be understood." — Elie Wiesel	*"A writer's job is not to judge but to seek to understand."* — Ernest Hemingway
October 9	**October 10**
"Writing is a form of therapy; sometimes I wonder how all those who do not write, compose, or paint can manage to escape the madness."	*"The most essential gift for a good writer is a built-in, shockproof crap detector."* — Ernest Hemingway

— Graham Greene

October 11

"I don't believe in writer's block. Think about it—when you were blocked in school and had to write a term paper, didn't it always manage to fix itself the night before?"

— Jodi Picoult

October 12

"When I'm writing, I know I'm doing the thing I was born to do."

— Anne Sexton

October 13

"Easy reading is damn hard writing."

— Nathaniel Hawthorne

October 14

"I write because I have to. Because the stories are already written in my heart."

— Unknown

October 15

"If you take your writing seriously, readers will take it seriously too."

— Unknown

October 16

"To write well, express yourself like the common people, but think like a wise man."

— Aristotle

October 17

"Let your characters surprise you."

— E.M. Forster

October 18

"The greatest thing about writing is that you can do it anywhere."

— Unknown

October 19

"I start writing when I overcome my disgust with myself."

— Franz Kafka

October 20

"Writing is exploration; you start from nothing and learn as you go."

— E.L. Doctorow

October 21	October 22
"Ideas come from everywhere— dreams, walks, conversations, but mostly from reading." — Stephen King	*"I don't know what I think until I write it down."* — Joan Didion
October 23	**October 24**
"Write to write. Write because you need to write. Write to settle the rage within you." — Zadie Smith	*"Inspiration exists, but it has to find you working."* — Pablo Picasso
October 25	**October 26**
"Writing a novel is a terrible experience, during which the hair often falls out and the teeth decay." — Flannery O'Connor	*"Don't wait. The time will never be just right."* — Napoleon Hill
October 27	**October 28**
"Literature is the art of discovering something extraordinary about ordinary people." — Boris Pasternak	*"Each draft takes you deeper into the story."* — Unknown
October 29	**October 30**
"There is a vitality, a life force, an energy, a quickening that is translated through you into action, and because there is only one of you in all time, this expression is unique." — Martha Graham	*"A good writer possesses not only their own spirit but also the spirit of their friends."* — Friedrich Nietzsche

October 31

"The reason 99% of all stories written are not bought by editors is very simple. Editors never buy manuscripts that are left in the bottom desk drawer at home."

— Isaac Asimov

October Social Media Planning

Monthly Social Media Goals & Tracking

Platform	Goal Posts	Completed	Content Ideas / Notes
Instagram	____	____	
Facebook	____	____	
TikTok	____	____	
BlueSky	____	____	
Threads	____	____	
LinkedIn	____	____	
YouTube/Shorts	____	____	
Pinterest	____	____	
Goodreads	____	____	
BookBub	____	____	
Author Website/Blog	____	____	

Weekly Social Media Content Calendar:

- Week 1: Behind-the-scenes character/plot development
- Week 2: Writing progress updates, word count milestones
- Week 3: First draft completion celebration, cover reveals

- Week 4: Book announcement, pre-order/launch details, contest entries

October Contest & Promotional Opportunities

Track submissions and deadlines

Contest/Opportunity	Deadline	Status	Entry Fee	Notes/Requirements
		☐ Plan ☐ Submit ☐ Done	$____	
		☐ Plan ☐ Submit ☐ Done	$____	
		☐ Plan ☐ Submit ☐ Done	$____	
		☐ Plan ☐ Submit ☐ Done	$____	
		☐ Plan ☐ Submit ☐ Done	$____	
		☐ Plan ☐ Submit ☐ Done	$____	
		☐ Plan ☐ Submit ☐ Done	$____	
		☐ Plan ☐ Submit ☐ Done	$____	
		☐ Plan ☐ Submit ☐ Done	$____	
		☐ Plan ☐ Submit ☐ Done	$____	

Promotional Opportunities Checklist:

- ☐ Book review blogs and websites
- ☐ BookTok/Bookstagram influencer outreach
- ☐ Goodreads giveaway or promotion
- ☐ BookBub featured deal submission
- ☐ Amazon/KDP advertising campaign
- ☐ Author newsletter announcement
- ☐ Podcast interview pitches
- ☐ Local bookstore/library events
- ☐ Cross-promotion with other authors
- ☐ Book club outreach

Stage Guide:

- Planning - Outlining, research, character development
- Drafting - Active writing phase
- Revising - Content editing and restructuring
- Editing - Line editing and polishing
- Publishing Prep - Cover design, formatting, contest submissions
- Published - Promotion and marketing phase

Week 1 (October 1-7): Writing Week

Primary Book Weekly Task Checklist:

PLANNING & SETUP (Days 1-3):

- ☐ Develop main characters (names, traits, motivations, arcs)
- ☐ Create basic plot outline or beat sheet
- ☐ Define key settings and world-building elements
- ☐ Research any necessary details for authenticity

WRITING BEGINS (Days 4-7):

- ☐ Write opening chapters (aim for 25% of target word count)
- ☐ Daily word/page count goal: _____ words/pages per day
- ☐ Establish narrative voice and tone
- ☐ Research 2-3 potential contests to enter

Date	Primary Book Progress	Other Books & Tasks	Social Media	Contests & Promos
Thu Oct 1	Words/pages: _____	Book 2: Book 3: Book 4: Book 5:	☐ IG ☐ FB ☐ TikTok ☐ BlueSky ☐ Threads ☐ YT ☐ Blog ☐ Other Prompt: ☐ Halloween book recommendations _____	☐ Research ☐ Prepare entry ☐ Submit _____

Date	Primary Book Progress	Other Books & Tasks	Social Media	Contests & Promos
Fri Oct 2	Words/pages: _____	Book 2: Book 3: Book 4: Book 5:	☐ IG ☐ FB ☐ TikTok ☐ BlueSky ☐ Threads ☐ YT ☐ Blog ☐ Other	☐ Research ☐ Prepare entry ☐ Submit
Sat Oct 3	Words/pages: _____ authenticity	Book 2: Book 3: Book 4: Book 5:	☐ IG ☐ FB ☐ TikTok ☐ BlueSky ☐ Threads ☐ YT ☐ Blog ☐ Other	☐ Research ☐ Prepare entry ☐ Submit
Sun Oct 4	Words/pages: _____	Book 2: Book 3: Book 4: Book 5:	☐ IG ☐ FB ☐ TikTok ☐ BlueSky ☐ Threads ☐ YT ☐ Blog ☐ Other	☐ Research ☐ Prepare entry ☐ Submit

Date	Primary Book Progress	Other Books & Tasks	Social Media	Contests & Promos
Mon Oct 5	Words/pages: _____	Book 2: Book 3: Book 4: Book 5:	☐ IG ☐ FB ☐ TikTok ☐ BlueSky ☐ Threads ☐ YT ☐ Blog ☐ Other _____	☐ Research ☐ Prepare entry ☐ Submit _____
Tue Oct 6	Words/pages: _____	Book 2: Book 3: Book 4: Book 5:	☐ IG ☐ FB ☐ TikTok ☐ BlueSky ☐ Threads ☐ YT ☐ Blog ☐ Other _____	☐ Research ☐ Prepare entry ☐ Submit _____
Wed Oct 7	Words/pages: _____	Book 2: Book 3: Book 4: Book 5:	☐ IG ☐ FB ☐ TikTok ☐ BlueSky ☐ Threads ☐ YT ☐ Blog ☐ Other _____	☐ Research ☐ Prepare entry ☐ Submit _____

Notes:

_____

_____

_____

Week 2 (October 8-14): Writing Week

Primary Book Weekly Task Checklist:

INTENSIVE WRITING WEEK:

- ☐ Write middle section chapters (aim for 40-50% of total manuscript)
- ☐ Daily word/page count goal: _____ words/pages per day
- ☐ Build tension and develop character relationships
- ☐ Keep notes on continuity issues to fix later
- ☐ Don't edit yet - focus on getting words on the page

MARKETING PREP:

- ☐ Draft social media posts about your writing progress
- ☐ Start thinking about cover concepts

Date	Primary Book Progress	Other Books & Tasks	Social Media	Contests & Promos
Thu Oct 8	Words/pages: _____	Book 2: Book 3: Book 4: Book 5:	☐ IG ☐ FB ☐ TikTok ☐ BlueSky ☐ Threads ☐ YT ☐ Blog ☐ Other Prompt: ☐ Scariest scene you've written	☐ Research ☐ Prepare entry ☐ Submit _____

Date	Primary Book Progress	Other Books & Tasks	Social Media	Contests & Promos
Fri Oct 9	Words/pages: _____	Book 2: Book 3: Book 4: Book 5:	☐ IG ☐ FB ☐ TikTok ☐ BlueSky ☐ Threads ☐ YT ☐ Blog ☐ Other _____	☐ Research ☐ Prepare entry ☐ Submit _____
Sat Oct 10	Words/pages: _____	Book 2: Book 3: Book 4: Book 5:	☐ IG ☐ FB ☐ TikTok ☐ BlueSky ☐ Threads ☐ YT ☐ Blog ☐ Other _____	☐ Research ☐ Prepare entry ☐ Submit _____
Sun Oct 11	Words/pages: _____	Book 2: Book 3: Book 4: Book 5:	☐ IG ☐ FB ☐ TikTok ☐ BlueSky ☐ Threads ☐ YT ☐ Blog ☐ Other _____	☐ Research ☐ Prepare entry ☐ Submit _____ _____

Date	Primary Book Progress	Other Books & Tasks	Social Media	Contests & Promos
Mon Oct 12	Words/pages: _____	Book 2: Book 3: Book 4: Book 5:	☐ IG ☐ FB ☐ TikTok ☐ BlueSky ☐ Threads ☐ YT ☐ Blog ☐ Other _____	☐ Research ☐ Prepare entry ☐ Submit _____
Tue Oct 13	Words/pages: _____	Book 2: Book 3: Book 4: Book 5:	☐ IG ☐ FB ☐ TikTok ☐ BlueSky ☐ Threads ☐ YT ☐ Blog ☐ Other _____	☐ Research ☐ Prepare entry ☐ Submit _____
Wed Oct 14	Words/pages: _____	Book 2: Book 3: Book 4: Book 5:	☐ IG ☐ FB ☐ TikTok ☐ BlueSky ☐ Threads ☐ YT ☐ Blog ☐ Other Prompt: ☐ Gothic/dark aesthetic posts _____	☐ Research ☐ Prepare entry ☐ Submit _____

287

☐ **Keep notes on continuity issues to fix later**

_____

_____

_____

_____

_____

_____

_____

_____

_____

_____

_____

_____

_____

_____

_____

_____

_____

Week 3 (October 15-21): Writing Week

Primary Book Weekly Task Checklist:

FINISH FIRST DRAFT:

- ☐ Complete remaining chapters and conclusion
- ☐ Daily word/page count goal: _____ words/pages per day
- ☐ Write climax and resolution
- ☐ Ensure all plot threads are addressed
- ☐ Celebrate completing first draft!

PREPARATION FOR NEXT WEEK:

- ☐ Let manuscript rest for 1-2 days if possible
- ☐ Begin cover design research and mockups
- ☐ Finalize contest submission list

Date	Primary Book Progress	Other Books & Tasks	Social Media	Contests & Promos
Thu Oct 15	Words/pages: _____	Book 2: Book 3: Book 4: Book 5:	☐ IG ☐ FB ☐ TikTok ☐ BlueSky ☐ Threads ☐ YT ☐ Blog ☐ Other Prompt: ☐ Thriller/ mystery excerpts _____ —	☐ Research ☐ Prepare entry ☐ Submit _____

Date	Primary Book Progress	Other Books & Tasks	Social Media	Contests & Promos
Fri Oct 16	Words/pages: _____	Book 2: Book 3: Book 4: Book 5:	☐ IG ☐ FB ☐ TikTok ☐ BlueSky ☐ Threads ☐ YT ☐ Blog ☐ Other _____	☐ Research ☐ Prepare entry ☐ Submit _____
Sat Oct 17	Words/pages: _____	Book 2: Book 3: Book 4: Book 5:	☐ IG ☐ FB ☐ TikTok ☐ BlueSky ☐ Threads ☐ YT ☐ Blog ☐ Other _____	☐ Research ☐ Prepare entry ☐ Submit _____
Sun Oct 18	Words/pages: _____	Book 2: Book 3: Book 4: Book 5:	☐ IG ☐ FB ☐ TikTok ☐ BlueSky ☐ Threads ☐ YT ☐ Blog ☐ Other _____	☐ Research ☐ Prepare entry ☐ Submit _____

Date	Primary Book Progress	Other Books & Tasks	Social Media	Contests & Promos
Mon Oct 19	Words/pages: _____	Book 2: Book 3: Book 4: Book 5:	☐ IG ☐ FB ☐ TikTok ☐ BlueSky ☐ Threads ☐ YT ☐ Blog ☐ Other _____	☐ Research ☐ Prepare entry ☐ Submit _____
Tue Oct 20	Words/pages: _____	Book 2: Book 3: Book 4: Book 5:	☐ IG ☐ FB ☐ TikTok ☐ BlueSky ☐ Threads ☐ YT ☐ Blog ☐ Other _____	☐ Research ☐ Prepare entry ☐ Submit _____
Wed Oct 21	Words/pages: _____	Book 2: Book 3: Book 4: Book 5:	☐ IG ☐ FB ☐ TikTok ☐ BlueSky ☐ Threads ☐ YT ☐ Blog ☐ Other Prompt: ☐ Horror writing tips _____	☐ Research ☐ Prepare entry ☐ Submit _____

Plot thread and/or cover design notes:

_____

_____

_____

Notes:

Week 4 (October 22-31): Editing & Publishing Week

Primary Book Weekly Task Checklist:

EDITING (Days 1-3):

- ☐ Read through entire manuscript, make notes
- ☐ Fix plot holes and continuity errors
- ☐ Strengthen weak scenes and dialogue
- ☐ Cut unnecessary content, tighten prose
- ☐ Proofread for grammar, spelling, typos

COVER & FORMATTING (Days 4-5):

- ☐ Design book cover (Canva, Photoshop, or hire designer)
- ☐ Format manuscript for publication (ebook/print)
- ☐ Write book description/blurb
- ☐ Create author bio if needed

PUBLISHING & PROMOTION (Days 6-10):

- ☐ Upload to publishing platform (KDP, IngramSpark, etc.)
- ☐ Submit to contest(s): _____
- ☐ Submit to contest(s): _____
- ☐ Schedule social media announcement posts
- ☐ Update author website/portfolio
- ☐ Send to beta readers or reviewers

Date	Primary Book Progress	Other Books & Tasks	Social Media	Contests & Promos
Thu Oct 22	Words/pages: _____	Book 2: Book 3: Book 4: Book 5:	☐ IG ☐ FB ☐ TikTok ☐ BlueSky ☐ Threads ☐ YT ☐ Blog ☐ Other _____	☐ Research ☐ Prepare entry ☐ Submit _____

Date	Primary Book Progress	Other Books & Tasks	Social Media	Contests & Promos
Fri Oct 23	Words/pages: _____	Book 2: Book 3: Book 4: Book 5:	☐ IG ☐ FB ☐ TikTok ☐ BlueSky ☐ Threads ☐ YT ☐ Blog ☐ Other _____	☐ Research ☐ Prepare entry ☐ Submit _____
Sat Oct 24	Words/pages: _____	Book 2: Book 3: Book 4: Book 5:	☐ IG ☐ FB ☐ TikTok ☐ BlueSky ☐ Threads ☐ YT ☐ Blog ☐ Other _____	☐ Research ☐ Prepare entry ☐ Submit _____
Sun Oct 25	Words/pages: _____	Book 2: Book 3: Book 4: Book 5:	☐ IG ☐ FB ☐ TikTok ☐ BlueSky ☐ Threads ☐ YT ☐ Blog ☐ Other _____	☐ Research ☐ Prepare entry ☐ Submit _____

Date	Primary Book Progress	Other Books & Tasks	Social Media	Contests & Promos
Mon Oct 26	Words/pages: _____	Book 2: Book 3: Book 4: Book 5:	☐ IG ☐ FB ☐ TikTok ☐ BlueSky ☐ Threads ☐ YT ☐ Blog ☐ Other _____	☐ Research ☐ Prepare entry ☐ Submit _____
Tue Oct 27	Words/pages: _____	Book 2: Book 3: Book 4: Book 5:	☐ IG ☐ FB ☐ TikTok ☐ BlueSky ☐ Threads ☐ YT ☐ Blog ☐ Other _____	☐ Research ☐ Prepare entry ☐ Submit _____
Wed Oct 28	Words/pages: _____	Book 2: Book 3: Book 4: Book 5:	☐ IG ☐ FB ☐ TikTok ☐ BlueSky ☐ Threads ☐ YT ☐ Blog ☐ Other Prompt: ☐ Costume ideas from your characters _____	☐ Research ☐ Prepare entry ☐ Submit _____

295

Date	Primary Book Progress	Other Books & Tasks	Social Media	Contests & Promos
Thu Oct 29	Words/pages: _____	Book 2: Book 3: Book 4: Book 5:	☐ IG ☐ FB ☐ TikTok ☐ BlueSky ☐ Threads ☐ YT ☐ Blog ☐ Other _____	☐ Research ☐ Prepare entry ☐ Submit _____
Fri Oct 30	Words/pages: _____	Book 2: Book 3: Book 4: Book 5:	☐ IG ☐ FB ☐ TikTok ☐ BlueSky ☐ Threads ☐ YT ☐ Blog ☐ Other _____	☐ Research ☐ Prepare entry ☐ Submit _____
Sat Oct 31	Words/pages: _____	Book 2: Book 3: Book 4: Book 5:	☐ IG ☐ FB ☐ TikTok ☐ BlueSky ☐ Threads ☐ YT ☐ Blog ☐ Other _____	☐ Research ☐ Prepare entry ☐ Submit _____

Notes:

_____

_____

_____

Designed by Jody Ortiz

October Review & Reflection

Primary Book Progress:

Status: ☐ Completed ☐ In Progress ☐ On Hold

Words/Pages Written This Month: _____

Progress on Other Books:

Book 2:
_____

Book 3:
_____

Book 4:
_____

Book 5:
_____

What worked well this month:

_____

_____

_____

_____

Challenges and solutions:

_____

_____

_____

_____

November 2026

Book to complete this month: _____

Genre: _____

Target Word/Page Count: _____

Current Stage: _____

Stage Guide:

- Planning - Outlining, research, character development

- Drafting - Active writing phase

- Revising - Content editing and restructuring

- Editing - Line editing and polishing

- Publishing Prep - Cover design, formatting, contest submissions

- Published - Promotion and marketing phase

Monthly Goals:
- Complete manuscript by day 21
- Finish editing and revisions by day 28
- Design professional cover
- Submit to at least 2 contests or promotional opportunities
- Post on social media 3x per week minimum
- _____
- _____

November 2026 - Projects Overview

Track up to 5 books in progress this month

Book	Title & Genre	Current Stage	Target Words/Pages	Month Goal
PRIMARY				
Book 2				
Book 3				
Book 4				
Book 5				

Book Color Coding Guide: Add highlighters or other shading for quick reference.

Book	Shading/Highlight Reference
PRIMARY (Book 1)	
Book 2	
Book 3	
Book 4	
Book 5	

November writing inspiration at a glance: Add these to your calendar or tape them to your computer or wherever they will inspire you.

November 1 *"If you haven't surprised yourself, you haven't written."* — Eudora Welty	**November 2** *"Stories are a communal currency of humanity."* — Tahir Shah
November 3 *"Writing is an underestimated art. You have to do so much in so little."* — Zadie Smith	**November 4** *"Great things are done by a series of small things brought together.'"* — Vincent van Gogh
November 5 *"You write your first draft with your heart, and you rewrite with your head."* — William Forrester	**November 6** *"Writing is medicine. It is an appropriate antidote to injury."* — Julia Cameron
November 7 *"The unexamined life is not worth living, and the unlived life is not worth examining."* — Unknown	**November 8** *"Write without pay until somebody offers to pay you. If nobody offers within three years, sawing wood is what you were intended for."* — Mark Twain
November 9 *"Sometimes you have to go on when you don't feel like it, and sometimes you're doing good work when it feels like all you're managing is to shovel aside the same lump of dirt."* — Stephen King	**November 10** *"All the information you need can be given in dialogue."* — Elmore Leonard

November 11

"Never use the word 'suddenly' just to create tension."

— Elmore Leonard

November 12

"Description is hard. Remember that all description is an opinion about the world."

— Anne Enright

November 13

"A writer is not so much someone who has something to say as they are someone who has found a process that will bring about new things they would not have thought of."

— William Stafford

November 14

"You must write for children in the same way as you do for adults, only better."

— Maxim Gorky

November 15

"The most valuable of all talents is never using two words when one will do."

— Thomas Jefferson

November 16

"Here is a lesson in creative writing: First rule, do not use semicolons."

— Kurt Vonnegut

November 17

"The universe is made of stories, not of atoms."

— Muriel Rukeyser

November 18

"A word is dead when it is said, some say. I say it just begins to live that day."

— Emily Dickinson

November 19

"We tell ourselves stories in order to live."

— Joan Didion

November 20

"To me, the greatest pleasure of writing is not what it's about, but the music the words make."

— Truman Capote

November 21	November 22
"Writing isn't about making money or becoming famous. Writing is about enriching the lives of yourself and others." — Unknown	*"I write to stay alive."* — Jamaica Kincaid

November 23	November 24
"The more closely the author thinks of why they wrote, the more they come to regard themselves as a kind of instrument." — Rainer Maria Rilke	*"Write what disturbs you, what you fear, what you have not been willing to speak about."* — Natalie Goldberg

November 25	November 26
"A successful book is not made of what is in it, but what is left out of it." — Mark Twain	*"When all else fails, write what your heart tells you."* — Unknown

November 27	November 28
"Metaphors have a way of holding the most truth in the least space." — Orson Scott Card	*"All readers come to fiction as willing accomplices to your lies."* — Steve Almond

November 29	November 30
"Every artist was first an amateur." — Ralph Waldo Emerson	*"Art washes away from the soul the dust of everyday life."* — Pablo Picasso

November Social Media Planning

Monthly Social Media Goals & Tracking

Platform	Goal Posts	Completed	Content Ideas / Notes
Instagram	____	____	
Facebook	____	____	
TikTok	____	____	
BlueSky	____	____	
Threads	____	____	
LinkedIn	____	____	
YouTube/Shorts	____	____	
Pinterest	____	____	
Goodreads	____	____	
BookBub	____	____	
Author Website/Blog	____	____	

Weekly Social Media Content Calendar:

- Week 1: Behind-the-scenes character/plot development
- Week 2: Writing progress updates, word count milestones
- Week 3: First draft completion celebration, cover reveals

305

- Week 4: Book announcement, pre-order/launch details, contest entries

November Contest & Promotional Opportunities

Track submissions and deadlines

Contest/Opportunity	Deadline	Status	Entry Fee	Notes/Requirements
		☐ Plan ☐ Submit ☐ Done	$____	
		☐ Plan ☐ Submit ☐ Done	$____	
		☐ Plan ☐ Submit ☐ Done	$____	
		☐ Plan ☐ Submit ☐ Done	$____	
		☐ Plan ☐ Submit ☐ Done	$____	
		☐ Plan ☐ Submit ☐ Done	$____	
		☐ Plan ☐ Submit ☐ Done	$____	
		☐ Plan ☐ Submit ☐ Done	$____	
		☐ Plan ☐ Submit ☐ Done	$____	
		☐ Plan ☐ Submit ☐ Done	$____	

Promotional Opportunities Checklist:

- ☐ Book review blogs and websites
- ☐ BookTok/Bookstagram influencer outreach
- ☐ Goodreads giveaway or promotion
- ☐ BookBub featured deal submission
- ☐ Amazon/KDP advertising campaign
- ☐ Author newsletter announcement
- ☐ Podcast interview pitches
- ☐ Local bookstore/library events
- ☐ Cross-promotion with other authors
- ☐ Book club outreach

Stage Guide:

- Planning - Outlining, research, character development
- Drafting - Active writing phase
- Revising - Content editing and restructuring
- Editing - Line editing and polishing
- Publishing Prep - Cover design, formatting, contest submissions
- Published - Promotion and marketing phase

Week 1 (November 1-7): Writing Week

Primary Book Weekly Task Checklist:

PLANNING & SETUP (Days 1-3):

- □ Develop main characters (names, traits, motivations, arcs)
- □ Create basic plot outline or beat sheet
- □ Define key settings and world-building elements
- □ Research any necessary details for authenticity

WRITING BEGINS (Days 4-7):

- □ Write opening chapters (aim for 25% of target word count)
- □ Daily word/page count goal: _____ words/pages per day
- □ Establish narrative voice and tone
- □ Research 2-3 potential contests to enter

Date	Primary Book Progress	Other Books & Tasks	Social Media	Contests & Promos
Sun Nov 1	Words/pages: _____	Book 2: Book 3: Book 4: Book 5:	□ IG □ FB □ TikTok □ BlueSky □ Threads □ YT □ Blog □ Other Prompt: □ Thankful for readers/ community	□ Research □ Prepare entry □ Submit _____

Date	Primary Book Progress	Other Books & Tasks	Social Media	Contests & Promos
Mon Nov 2	Words/pages: _____	Book 2: Book 3: Book 4: Book 5:	☐ IG ☐ FB ☐ TikTok ☐ BlueSky ☐ Threads ☐ YT ☐ Blog ☐ Other _____	☐ Research ☐ Prepare entry ☐ Submit _____
Tue Nov 3	Words/pages: _____	Book 2: Book 3: Book 4: Book 5:	☐ IG ☐ FB ☐ TikTok ☐ BlueSky ☐ Threads ☐ YT ☐ Blog ☐ Other _____	☐ Research ☐ Prepare entry ☐ Submit _____
Wed Nov 4	Words/pages: _____	Book 2: Book 3: Book 4: Book 5:	☐ IG ☐ FB ☐ TikTok ☐ BlueSky ☐ Threads ☐ YT ☐ Blog ☐ Other _____	☐ Research ☐ Prepare entry ☐ Submit _____

Designed by Jody Ortiz

Date	Primary Book Progress	Other Books & Tasks	Social Media	Contests & Promos
Thu Nov 5	Words/pages: _____	Book 2: Book 3: Book 4: Book 5:	☐ IG ☐ FB ☐ TikTok ☐ BlueSky ☐ Threads ☐ YT ☐ Blog ☐ Other _____	☐ Research ☐ Prepare entry ☐ Submit _____
Fri Nov 6	Words/pages: _____	Book 2: Book 3: Book 4: Book 5:	☐ IG ☐ FB ☐ TikTok ☐ BlueSky ☐ Threads ☐ YT ☐ Blog ☐ Other _____	☐ Research ☐ Prepare entry ☐ Submit _____
Sat Nov 7	Words/pages: _____	Book 2: Book 3: Book 4: Book 5:	☐ IG ☐ FB ☐ TikTok ☐ BlueSky ☐ Threads ☐ YT ☐ Blog ☐ Other Prompt: ☐ Writing sprint challenges _____	☐ Research ☐ Prepare entry ☐ Submit _____

Notes:

Week 2 (November 8-14): Writing Week

Primary Book Weekly Task Checklist:

INTENSIVE WRITING WEEK:

- ☐ Write middle section chapters (aim for 40-50% of total manuscript)
- ☐ Daily word/page count goal: _____ words/pages per day
- ☐ Build tension and develop character relationships
- ☐ Keep notes on continuity issues to fix later
- ☐ Don't edit yet - focus on getting words on the page

MARKETING PREP:

- ☐ Draft social media posts about your writing progress
- ☐ Start thinking about cover concepts

Date	Primary Book Progress	Other Books & Tasks	Social Media	Contests & Promos
Sun Nov 8	Words/pages: _____	Book 2: Book 3: Book 4: Book 5:	☐ IG ☐ FB ☐ TikTok ☐ BlueSky ☐ Threads ☐ YT ☐ Blog ☐ Other	☐ Research ☐ Prepare entry ☐ Submit

Date	Primary Book Progress	Other Books & Tasks	Social Media	Contests & Promos
Mon Nov 9	Words/pages: _____	Book 2: Book 3: Book 4: Book 5:	☐ IG ☐ FB ☐ TikTok ☐ BlueSky ☐ Threads ☐ YT ☐ Blog ☐ Other _____	☐ Research ☐ Prepare entry ☐ Submit _____
Tue Nov 10	Words/pages: _____	Book 2: Book 3: Book 4: Book 5:	☐ IG ☐ FB ☐ TikTok ☐ BlueSky ☐ Threads ☐ YT ☐ Blog ☐ Other Prompt: ☐ Thanksgiving book gift guide _____	☐ Research ☐ Prepare entry ☐ Submit _____
Wed Nov 11	Words/pages: _____	Book 2: Book 3: Book 4: Book 5:	☐ IG ☐ FB ☐ TikTok ☐ BlueSky ☐ Threads ☐ YT ☐ Blog ☐ Other _____	☐ Research ☐ Prepare entry ☐ Submit _____

Date	Primary Book Progress	Other Books & Tasks	Social Media	Contests & Promos
Thu Nov 12	Words/pages: _____	Book 2: Book 3: Book 4: Book 5:	☐ IG ☐ FB ☐ TikTok ☐ BlueSky ☐ Threads ☐ YT ☐ Blog ☐ Other _____	☐ Research ☐ Prepare entry ☐ Submit _____
Fri Nov 13	Words/pages: _____	Book 2: Book 3: Book 4: Book 5:	☐ IG ☐ FB ☐ TikTok ☐ BlueSky ☐ Threads ☐ YT ☐ Blog ☐ Other _____	☐ Research ☐ Prepare entry ☐ Submit _____
Sat Nov 14	Words/pages: _____	Book 2: Book 3: Book 4: Book 5:	☐ IG ☐ FB ☐ TikTok ☐ BlueSky ☐ Threads ☐ YT ☐ Blog ☐ Other _____	☐ Research ☐ Prepare entry ☐ Submit _____

☐ Keep notes on continuity issues to fix later

_____
_____
_____
_____
_____
_____
_____
_____
_____
_____
_____
_____
_____
_____
_____
_____
_____
_____

Week 3 (November 15-21): Writing Week

Primary Book Weekly Task Checklist:

FINISH FIRST DRAFT:

- ☐ Complete remaining chapters and conclusion
- ☐ Daily word/page count goal: _____ words/pages per day
- ☐ Write climax and resolution
- ☐ Ensure all plot threads are addressed
- ☐ Celebrate completing first draft!

PREPARATION FOR NEXT WEEK:

- ☐ Let manuscript rest for 1-2 days if possible
- ☐ Begin cover design research and mockups
- ☐ Finalize contest submission list

Date	Primary Book Progress	Other Books & Tasks	Social Media	Contests & Promos
Sun Nov 15	Words/pages: _____	Book 2: Book 3: Book 4: Book 5:	☐ IG ☐ FB ☐ TikTok ☐ BlueSky ☐ Threads ☐ YT ☐ Blog ☐ Other Prompt: ☐ Author friends shoutouts	☐ Research ☐ Prepare entry ☐ Submit _____

Date	Primary Book Progress	Other Books & Tasks	Social Media	Contests & Promos
Mon Nov 16	Words/pages: _____	Book 2: Book 3: Book 4: Book 5:	☐ IG ☐ FB ☐ TikTok ☐ BlueSky ☐ Threads ☐ YT ☐ Blog ☐ Other _____	☐ Research ☐ Prepare entry ☐ Submit _____
Tue Nov 17	Words/pages: _____	Book 2: Book 3: Book 4: Book 5:	☐ IG ☐ FB ☐ TikTok ☐ BlueSky ☐ Threads ☐ YT ☐ Blog ☐ Other _____	☐ Research ☐ Prepare entry ☐ Submit _____
Wed Nov 18	Words/pages: _____	Book 2: Book 3: Book 4: Book 5:	☐ IG ☐ FB ☐ TikTok ☐ BlueSky ☐ Threads ☐ YT ☐ Blog ☐ Other _____	☐ Research ☐ Prepare entry ☐ Submit _____

317

Date	Primary Book Progress	Other Books & Tasks	Social Media	Contests & Promos
Thu Nov 19	Words/pages: _____	Book 2: Book 3: Book 4: Book 5:	☐ IG ☐ FB ☐ TikTok ☐ BlueSky ☐ Threads ☐ YT ☐ Blog ☐ Other _____	☐ Research ☐ Prepare entry ☐ Submit _____
Fri Nov 20	Words/pages: _____	Book 2: Book 3: Book 4: Book 5:	☐ IG ☐ FB ☐ TikTok ☐ BlueSky ☐ Threads ☐ YT ☐ Blog ☐ Other _____	☐ Research ☐ Prepare entry ☐ Submit _____
Sat Nov 21	Words/pages: _____	Book 2: Book 3: Book 4: Book 5:	☐ IG ☐ FB ☐ TikTok ☐ BlueSky ☐ Threads ☐ YT ☐ Blog ☐ Other _____	☐ Research ☐ Prepare entry ☐ Submit _____

Plot thread and/or cover design notes:

_____

_____

_____

Notes:

Week 4 (November 22-30): Editing & Publishing Week

Primary Book Weekly Task Checklist:

EDITING (Days 1-3):

- ☐ Read through entire manuscript, make notes
- ☐ Fix plot holes and continuity errors
- ☐ Strengthen weak scenes and dialogue
- ☐ Cut unnecessary content, tighten prose
- ☐ Proofread for grammar, spelling, typos

COVER & FORMATTING (Days 4-5):

- ☐ Design book cover (Canva, Photoshop, or hire designer)
- ☐ Format manuscript for publication (ebook/print)
- ☐ Write book description/blurb
- ☐ Create author bio if needed

PUBLISHING & PROMOTION (Days 6-9):

- ☐ Upload to publishing platform (KDP, IngramSpark, etc.)
- ☐ Submit to contest(s): _____
- ☐ Submit to contest(s): _____
- ☐ Schedule social media announcement posts
- ☐ Update author website/portfolio
- ☐ Send to beta readers or reviewers

Date	Primary Book Progress	Other Books & Tasks	Social Media	Contests & Promos
Sun Nov 22	Words/pages: _____	Book 2: Book 3: Book 4: Book 5:	☐ IG ☐ FB ☐ TikTok ☐ BlueSky ☐ Threads ☐ YT ☐ Blog ☐ Other _____	☐ Research ☐ Prepare entry ☐ Submit _____
Mon Nov 23	Words/pages: _____	Book 2: Book 3: Book 4: Book 5:	☐ IG ☐ FB ☐ TikTok ☐ BlueSky ☐ Threads ☐ YT ☐ Blog ☐ Other Prompt: ☐ Author friends shoutouts	☐ Research ☐ Prepare entry ☐ Submit _____
Tue Nov 24	Words/pages: _____	Book 2: Book 3: Book 4: Book 5:	☐ IG ☐ FB ☐ TikTok ☐ BlueSky ☐ Threads ☐ YT ☐ Blog ☐ Other _____	☐ Research ☐ Prepare entry ☐ Submit _____

Date	Primary Book Progress	Other Books & Tasks	Social Media	Contests & Promos
Wed Nov 25	Words/pages: _____	Book 2: Book 3: Book 4: Book 5:	☐ IG ☐ FB ☐ TikTok ☐ BlueSky ☐ Threads ☐ YT ☐ Blog ☐ Other _____	☐ Research ☐ Prepare entry ☐ Submit
Thu Nov 26	Words/pages: _____	Book 2: Book 3: Book 4: Book 5:	☐ IG ☐ FB ☐ TikTok ☐ BlueSky ☐ Threads ☐ YT ☐ Blog ☐ Other _____	☐ Research ☐ Prepare entry ☐ Submit _____
Fri Nov 27	Words/pages: _____	Book 2: Book 3: Book 4: Book 5:	☐ IG ☐ FB ☐ TikTok ☐ BlueSky ☐ Threads ☐ YT ☐ Blog ☐ Other _____	☐ Research ☐ Prepare entry ☐ Submit _____

Date	Primary Book Progress	Other Books & Tasks	Social Media	Contests & Promos
Sat Nov 28	Words/pages: _____	Book 2: Book 3: Book 4: Book 5:	☐ IG ☐ FB ☐ TikTok ☐ BlueSky ☐ Threads ☐ YT ☐ Blog ☐ Other Prompt: ☐ Word count victory celebrations	☐ Research ☐ Prepare entry ☐ Submit _____
Sun Nov 29	Words/pages: _____	Book 2: Book 3: Book 4: Book 5:	☐ IG ☐ FB ☐ TikTok ☐ BlueSky ☐ Threads ☐ YT ☐ Blog ☐ Other _____	☐ Research ☐ Prepare entry ☐ Submit _____
Mon Nov 30	Words/pages: _____	Book 2: Book 3: Book 4: Book 5:	☐ IG ☐ FB ☐ TikTok ☐ BlueSky ☐ Threads ☐ YT ☐ Blog ☐ Other _____	☐ Research ☐ Prepare entry ☐ Submit _____

Notes:

_____

_____

Designed by Jody Ortiz

November Review & Reflection

Primary Book Progress:

Status: ☐ Completed   ☐ In Progress   ☐ On Hold

Words/Pages Written This Month: _____

Progress on Other Books:

Book 2:
_____

Book 3:
_____

Book 4:
_____

Book 5:
_____

What worked well this month:

_____

_____

_____

_____

Challenges and solutions:

_____

_____

_____

_____

December 2026

Book to complete this month: _____

Genre: _____

Target Word/Page Count: _____

Current Stage: _____

Stage Guide:

- Planning - Outlining, research, character development

- Drafting - Active writing phase

- Revising - Content editing and restructuring

- Editing - Line editing and polishing

- Publishing Prep - Cover design, formatting, contest submissions

- Published - Promotion and marketing phase

Monthly Goals:
- Complete manuscript by day 21
- Finish editing and revisions by day 28
- Design professional cover
- Submit to at least 2 contests or promotional opportunities
- Post on social media 3x per week minimum
- _____
- _____

December 2026 - Projects Overview

Track up to 5 books in progress this month

Book	Title & Genre	Current Stage	Target Words/Pages	Month Goal
PRIMARY				
Book 2				
Book 3				
Book 4				
Book 5				

Book Color Coding Guide: Add highlighters or other shading for quick reference.

Book	Shading/Highlight Reference
PRIMARY (Book 1)	
Book 2	
Book 3	
Book 4	
Book 5	

December writing inspiration at a glance: Add these to your calendar or tape them to your computer or wherever they will inspire you.

December 1 *"The miracle is not to walk on water. The miracle is to walk on the green earth, dwelling deeply in the present moment."* — Thích Nhất Hạnh	**December 2** *"Writing is the only thing that passes the three tests of merit: it is honest, useful, and beautiful."* — Unknown
December 3 *"I write because not to write is inconceivable."* — Philip Roth	**December 4** *"Stories are how we think. They are how we make meaning of life."* — Chimamanda Ngozi Adichie
December 5 *"Writers remember everything, especially the hurts. Strip a writer to the buff, point to the scars, and they'll tell you the story of each small one."* — Janet Fitch	**December 6** *"Writing, at its best, is a lonely life."* — Ernest Hemingway
December 7 *"Everybody walks past a thousand story ideas every day. The good writers are the ones who see five or six of them."* — Orson Scott Card	**December 8** *"If I waited for perfection, I would never write a word."* — Margaret Atwood

December 9

"You must be willing to do the things today that others won't do, in order to have the things tomorrow that others won't have."

— Les Brown

December 10

"A writer is always working, even when they are staring out the window."

— Unknown

December 11

"Don't wait for inspiration. It comes while working."

— Henri Matisse

December 12

"We read to know we're not alone."

— William Nicholson

December 13

"Writing is a dog's life, but the only life worth living."

— Gustave Flaubert

December 14

"You never know what's around the corner. It could be everything. Or it could be nothing. You keep putting one foot in front of the other."

— Tom Hanks

December 15

"Your manuscript is both good and original. But the part that is good is not original, and the part that is original is not good."

— Samuel Johnson

December 16

"When something can be read without effort, great effort has gone into its writing."

— Enrique Jardiel Poncela

December 17

"I can shake off everything as I write; my sorrows disappear, my courage is reborn."

— Anne Frank

December 18

"The job is to ask questions—it always was—and to ask them as inexorably as I can."

— Arthur Miller

December 19

"Your story is what you have, what you will always have. It is something to own."
— Michelle Obama

December 20

"Writers are grown-ups with imaginary friends living in their heads."
— Jody Ortiz

December 21

"Don't get it right, just get it written."
— James Thurber

December 22

"The only bad writing is no writing at all."
— Unknown

December 23

"There is no friend as loyal as a book."
— Ernest Hemingway

December 24

"Writing is a solitary journey, but we're all on this road together."
— Unknown

December 25

"I get my best ideas when I have nowhere to write them."
— Jody Ortiz

December 26

"If you don't have the time to read, you don't have the time or the tools to write."
— Stephen King

December 27

"Your time is limited, don't waste it living someone else's life."
— Steve Jobs

December 28

"Write the ending first, then write toward it."
— Unknown

December 29

"Change will not come if we wait for some other person or some other time. We are the ones we've been waiting for. We are the change that we seek."
— Barack Obama

December 30

"Stories are your imaginary friends coming to life in someone else's head."
— Jody Ortiz

December 31

"We did not come to fear the future. We came to shape it."
— Barack Obama

December Social Media Planning

Monthly Social Media Goals & Tracking

Platform	Goal Posts	Completed	Content Ideas / Notes
Instagram	____	____	
Facebook	____	____	
TikTok	____	____	
BlueSky	____	____	
Threads	____	____	
LinkedIn	____	____	
YouTube/Shorts	____	____	
Pinterest	____	____	
Goodreads	____	____	
BookBub	____	____	
Author Website/Blog	____	____	

Weekly Social Media Content Calendar:

- Week 1: Behind-the-scenes character/plot development
- Week 2: Writing progress updates, word count milestones
- Week 3: First draft completion celebration, cover reveals

333

- Week 4: Book announcement, pre-order/launch details, contest entries

December Contest & Promotional Opportunities

Track submissions and deadlines

Contest/Opportunity	Deadline	Status	Entry Fee	Notes/Requirements
		☐ Plan ☐ Submit ☐ Done	$____	
		☐ Plan ☐ Submit ☐ Done	$____	
		☐ Plan ☐ Submit ☐ Done	$____	
		☐ Plan ☐ Submit ☐ Done	$____	
		☐ Plan ☐ Submit ☐ Done	$____	
		☐ Plan ☐ Submit ☐ Done	$____	
		☐ Plan ☐ Submit ☐ Done	$____	
		☐ Plan ☐ Submit ☐ Done	$____	
		☐ Plan ☐ Submit ☐ Done	$____	
		☐ Plan ☐ Submit ☐ Done	$____	

Promotional Opportunities Checklist:

- ☐ Book review blogs and websites
- ☐ BookTok/Bookstagram influencer outreach
- ☐ Goodreads giveaway or promotion
- ☐ BookBub featured deal submission
- ☐ Amazon/KDP advertising campaign
- ☐ Author newsletter announcement
- ☐ Podcast interview pitches
- ☐ Local bookstore/library events
- ☐ Cross-promotion with other authors
- ☐ Book club outreach

Stage Guide:

- Planning - Outlining, research, character development
- Drafting - Active writing phase
- Revising - Content editing and restructuring
- Editing - Line editing and polishing
- Publishing Prep - Cover design, formatting, contest submissions
- Published - Promotion and marketing phase

Week 1 (December 1-7): Writing Week

Primary Book Weekly Task Checklist:

PLANNING & SETUP (Days 1-3):

- ☐ Develop main characters (names, traits, motivations, arcs)
- ☐ Create basic plot outline or beat sheet
- ☐ Define key settings and world-building elements
- ☐ Research any necessary details for authenticity

WRITING BEGINS (Days 4-7):

- ☐ Write opening chapters (aim for 25% of target word count)
- ☐ Daily word/page count goal: _____ words/pages per day
- ☐ Establish narrative voice and tone
- ☐ Research 2-3 potential contests to enter

Date	Primary Book Progress	Other Books & Tasks	Social Media	Contests & Promos
Tue **Dec 1**	Words/pages: _____	Book 2: Book 3: Book 4: Book 5:	☐ IG ☐ FB ☐ TikTok ☐ BlueSky ☐ Threads ☐ YT ☐ Blog ☐ Other Prompt: ☐ Holiday book gift guide _____	☐ Research ☐ Prepare entry ☐ Submit _____

Date	Primary Book Progress	Other Books & Tasks	Social Media	Contests & Promos
Wed Dec 2	Words/pages: _____	Book 2: Book 3: Book 4: Book 5:	☐ IG ☐ FB ☐ TikTok ☐ BlueSky ☐ Threads ☐ YT ☐ Blog ☐ Other _____	☐ Research ☐ Prepare entry ☐ Submit _____
Thu Dec 3	Words/pages: _____	Book 2: Book 3: Book 4: Book 5:	☐ IG ☐ FB ☐ TikTok ☐ BlueSky ☐ Threads ☐ YT ☐ Blog ☐ Other _____	☐ Research ☐ Prepare entry ☐ Submit _____
Fri Dec 4	Words/pages: _____	Book 2: Book 3: Book 4: Book 5:	☐ IG ☐ FB ☐ TikTok ☐ BlueSky ☐ Threads ☐ YT ☐ Blog ☐ Other _____	☐ Research ☐ Prepare entry ☐ Submit _____

Date	Primary Book Progress	Other Books & Tasks	Social Media	Contests & Promos
Sat Dec 5	Words/pages: _____	Book 2: Book 3: Book 4: Book 5:	☐ IG ☐ FB ☐ TikTok ☐ BlueSky ☐ Threads ☐ YT ☐ Blog ☐ Other _____	☐ Research ☐ Prepare entry ☐ Submit _____
Sun Dec 6	Words/pages: _____	Book 2: Book 3: Book 4: Book 5:	☐ IG ☐ FB ☐ TikTok ☐ BlueSky ☐ Threads ☐ YT ☐ Blog ☐ Other _____	☐ Research ☐ Prepare entry ☐ Submit _____
Mon Dec 7	Words/pages: _____	Book 2: Book 3: Book 4: Book 5:	☐ IG ☐ FB ☐ TikTok ☐ BlueSky ☐ Threads ☐ YT ☐ Blog ☐ Other _____	☐ Research ☐ Prepare entry ☐ Submit _____

Notes:

_____

_____

_____

Week 2 (December 8-14): Writing Week

Primary Book Weekly Task Checklist:

INTENSIVE WRITING WEEK:

- ☐ Write middle section chapters (aim for 40-50% of total manuscript)
- ☐ Daily word/page count goal: _____ words/pages per day
- ☐ Build tension and develop character relationships
- ☐ Keep notes on continuity issues to fix later
- ☐ Don't edit yet - focus on getting words on the page

MARKETING PREP:

- ☐ Draft social media posts about your writing progress
- ☐ Start thinking about cover concepts

Date	Primary Book Progress	Other Books & Tasks	Social Media	Contests & Promos
Tue Dec 8	Words/pages: _____	Book 2: Book 3: Book 4: Book 5:	☐ IG ☐ FB ☐ TikTok ☐ BlueSky ☐ Threads ☐ YT ☐ Blog ☐ Other Prompt: ☐ Favorite writing moments of the year	☐ Research ☐ Prepare entry ☐ Submit

Date	Primary Book Progress	Other Books & Tasks	Social Media	Contests & Promos
Wed Dec 9	Words/pages: _____	Book 2: Book 3: Book 4: Book 5:	☐ IG ☐ FB ☐ TikTok ☐ BlueSky ☐ Threads ☐ YT ☐ Blog ☐ Other _____	☐ Research ☐ Prepare entry ☐ Submit _____
Thu Dec 10	Words/pages: _____	Book 2: Book 3: Book 4: Book 5:	☐ IG ☐ FB ☐ TikTok ☐ BlueSky ☐ Threads ☐ YT ☐ Blog ☐ Other _____	☐ Research ☐ Prepare entry ☐ Submit _____
Fri Dec 11	Words/pages: _____	Book 2: Book 3: Book 4: Book 5:	☐ IG ☐ FB ☐ TikTok ☐ BlueSky ☐ Threads ☐ YT ☐ Blog ☐ Other	☐ Research ☐ Prepare entry ☐ Submit _____

Designed by Jody Ortiz

Date	Primary Book Progress	Other Books & Tasks	Social Media	Contests & Promos
Sat Dec 12	Words/pages: _____	Book 2: Book 3: Book 4: Book 5:	☐ IG ☐ FB ☐ TikTok ☐ BlueSky ☐ Threads ☐ YT ☐ Blog ☐ Other _____	☐ Research ☐ Prepare entry ☐ Submit _____
Sun Dec 13	Words/pages: _____	Book 2: Book 3: Book 4: Book 5:	☐ IG ☐ FB ☐ TikTok ☐ BlueSky ☐ Threads ☐ YT ☐ Blog ☐ Other _____	☐ Research ☐ Prepare entry ☐ Submit _____
Mon Dec 14	Words/pages: _____	Book 2: Book 3: Book 4: Book 5:	☐ IG ☐ FB ☐ TikTok ☐ BlueSky ☐ Threads ☐ YT ☐ Blog ☐ Other _____	☐ Research ☐ Prepare entry ☐ Submit _____

☐ Keep notes on continuity issues to fix later

_____
_____
_____
_____
_____
_____
_____
_____
_____
_____
_____
_____
_____
_____
_____
_____

Week 3 (December 15-21): Writing Week

Primary Book Weekly Task Checklist:

FINISH FIRST DRAFT:

- ☐ Complete remaining chapters and conclusion
- ☐ Daily word/page count goal: _____ words/pages per day
- ☐ Write climax and resolution
- ☐ Ensure all plot threads are addressed
- ☐ Celebrate completing first draft!

PREPARATION FOR NEXT WEEK:

- ☐ Let manuscript rest for 1-2 days if possible
- ☐ Begin cover design research and mockups
- ☐ Finalize contest submission list

Date	Primary Book Progress	Other Books & Tasks	Social Media	Contests & Promos
Tue Dec 15	Words/pages: _____	Book 2: Book 3: Book 4: Book 5:	☐ IG ☐ FB ☐ TikTok ☐ BlueSky ☐ Threads ☐ YT ☐ Blog ☐ Other	☐ Research ☐ Prepare entry ☐ Submit

Date	Primary Book Progress	Other Books & Tasks	Social Media	Contests & Promos
Wed Dec 16	Words/pages: _____	Book 2: Book 3: Book 4: Book 5:	☐ IG ☐ FB ☐ TikTok ☐ BlueSky ☐ Threads ☐ YT ☐ Blog ☐ Other Prompt: ☐ Thank you to supporters _____	☐ Research ☐ Prepare entry ☐ Submit _____
Thu Dec 17	Words/pages: _____	Book 2: Book 3: Book 4: Book 5:	☐ IG ☐ FB ☐ TikTok ☐ BlueSky ☐ Threads ☐ YT ☐ Blog ☐ Other _____	☐ Research ☐ Prepare entry ☐ Submit _____
Fri Dec 18	Words/pages: _____	Book 2: Book 3: Book 4: Book 5:	☐ IG ☐ FB ☐ TikTok ☐ BlueSky ☐ Threads ☐ YT ☐ Blog ☐ Other _____	☐ Research ☐ Prepare entry ☐ Submit _____

345

Date	Primary Book Progress	Other Books & Tasks	Social Media	Contests & Promos
Sat Dec 19	Words/pages: _____	▩ Book 2: ▩ Book 3: ▩ Book 4: ▩ Book 5:	☐ IG ☐ FB ☐ TikTok ☐ BlueSky ☐ Threads ☐ YT ☐ Blog ☐ Other Prompt: ☐ New Year goals teaser _____	☐ Research ☐ Prepare entry ☐ Submit _____
Sun Dec 20	Words/pages: _____	▩ Book 2: ▩ Book 3: ▩ Book 4: ▩ Book 5:	☐ IG ☐ FB ☐ TikTok ☐ BlueSky ☐ Threads ☐ YT ☐ Blog ☐ Other _____	☐ Research ☐ Prepare entry ☐ Submit _____
Mon Dec 21	Words/pages: _____	▩ Book 2: ▩ Book 3: ▩ Book 4: ▩ Book 5:	☐ IG ☐ FB ☐ TikTok ☐ BlueSky ☐ Threads ☐ YT ☐ Blog ☐ Other _____	☐ Research ☐ Prepare entry ☐ Submit _____

Plot thread and/or cover design notes:

_____

_____

_____

Notes:

Week 4 (December 22-31): Editing & Publishing Week

Primary Book Weekly Task Checklist:

EDITING (Days 1-3):

- ☐ Read through entire manuscript, make notes
- ☐ Fix plot holes and continuity errors
- ☐ Strengthen weak scenes and dialogue
- ☐ Cut unnecessary content, tighten prose
- ☐ Proofread for grammar, spelling, typos

COVER & FORMATTING (Days 4-5):

- ☐ Design book cover (Canva, Photoshop, or hire designer)
- ☐ Format manuscript for publication (ebook/print)
- ☐ Write book description/blurb
- ☐ Create author bio if needed

PUBLISHING & PROMOTION (Days 6-10):

- ☐ Upload to publishing platform (KDP, IngramSpark, etc.)
- ☐ Submit to contest(s): _____
- ☐ Submit to contest(s): _____
- ☐ Schedule social media announcement posts
- ☐ Update author website/portfolio
- ☐ Send to beta readers or reviewers

Date	Primary Book Progress	Other Books & Tasks	Social Media	Contests & Promos
Tue Dec 22	Words/pages: _____	Book 2: _____ Book 3: _____ Book 4: _____ Book 5: _____	☐ IG ☐ FB ☐ TikTok ☐ BlueSky ☐ Threads ☐ YT ☐ Blog ☐ Other _____ _____	☐ Research ☐ Prepare entry ☐ Submit _____ _____

Date	Primary Book Progress	Other Books & Tasks	Social Media	Contests & Promos
Wed Dec 23	Words/pages: _____	Book 2: Book 3: Book 4: Book 5:	☐ IG ☐ FB ☐ TikTok ☐ BlueSky ☐ Threads ☐ YT ☐ Blog ☐ Other _____	☐ Research ☐ Prepare entry ☐ Submit _____
Thu Dec 24	Words/pages: _____	Book 2: Book 3: Book 4: Book 5:	☐ IG ☐ FB ☐ TikTok ☐ BlueSky ☐ Threads ☐ YT ☐ Blog ☐ Other _____ _____	☐ Research ☐ Prepare entry ☐ Submit _____ _____
Fri Dec 25	Words/pages: _____	Book 2: Book 3: Book 4: Book 5:	☐ IG ☐ FB ☐ TikTok ☐ BlueSky ☐ Threads ☐ YT ☐ Blog ☐ Other _____	☐ Research ☐ Prepare entry ☐ Submit _____

Date	Primary Book Progress	Other Books & Tasks	Social Media	Contests & Promos
Sat Dec 26	Words/pages: _____	Book 2: Book 3: Book 4: Book 5:	☐ IG ☐ FB ☐ TikTok ☐ BlueSky ☐ Threads ☐ YT ☐ Blog ☐ Other _____	☐ Research ☐ Prepare entry ☐ Submit _____
Sun Dec 27	Words/pages: _____	Book 2: Book 3: Book 4: Book 5:	☐ IG ☐ FB ☐ TikTok ☐ BlueSky ☐ Threads ☐ YT ☐ Blog ☐ Other _____	☐ Research ☐ Prepare entry ☐ Submit _____
Mon Dec 28	Words/pages: _____	Book 2: Book 3: Book 4: Book 5:	☐ IG ☐ FB ☐ TikTok ☐ BlueSky ☐ Threads ☐ YT ☐ Blog ☐ Other _____	☐ Research ☐ Prepare entry ☐ Submit _____

Date	Primary Book Progress	Other Books & Tasks	Social Media	Contests & Promos
Tue Dec 29	Words/pages: _____	Book 2: Book 3: Book 4: Book 5:	□ IG □ FB □ TikTok □ BlueSky □ Threads □ YT □ Blog □ Other _____	□ Research □ Prepare entry □ Submit _____
Wed Dec 30	Words/pages: _____	Book 2: Book 3: Book 4: Book 5:	□ IG □ FB □ TikTok □ BlueSky □ Threads □ YT □ Blog □ Other _____	□ Research □ Prepare entry □ Submit _____
Thu Dec 31	Words/pages: _____	Book 2: Book 3: Book 4: Book 5:	□ IG □ FB □ TikTok □ BlueSky □ Threads □ YT □ Blog □ Other _____	□ Research □ Prepare entry □ Submit _____

Notes:

_____

_____

_____

December Review & Reflection

Primary Book Progress:

Status: ☐ Completed ☐ In Progress ☐ On Hold

Words/Pages Written This Month: _____

Progress on Other Books:

Book 2:
_____

Book 3:
_____

Book 4:
_____

Book 5:
_____

What worked well this month:

_____
_____
_____
_____

Challenges and solutions:

_____
_____
_____
_____

Q4 2026

October - December

OCTOBER	NOVEMBER	DECEMBER
BOOK 1	BOOK 1	BOOK 1
Title:	Title:	Title:
_____	_____	_____
Genre:	Genre:	Genre:
_____	_____	_____
Status:	Status:	Status:
_____	_____	_____
BOOK 2	BOOK 2	BOOK 2
Title:	Title:	Title:
_____	_____	_____
Genre:	Genre:	Genre:
_____	_____	_____
Status:	Status:	Status:
_____	_____	_____
BOOK 3	BOOK 3	BOOK 3
Title:	Title:	Title:
_____	_____	_____
Genre:	Genre:	Genre:
_____	_____	_____
Status:	Status:	Status:
_____	_____	_____

Q4 KEY DEADLINES & MILESTONES

_____
_____
_____
_____
_____
_____
_____
_____
_____
_____
_____

Q4 REFLECTIONS & WINS

_____
_____
_____
_____
_____
_____

2026 Year-End Review

Total Books Completed in 2026: _____

Total Words/Pages Written: _____

Books Published:

1. _____
2. _____
3. _____
4. _____
5. _____
6. _____
7. _____
8. _____
9. _____
10. _____
11. _____
12. _____
13. _____
14. _____

Contests Won or Placed:

_____
_____
_____
_____
_____
_____
_____
_____
_____
_____
_____
_____
_____

_____
_____
_____
_____
_____

List of all books worked on in 2026:

1. _____
2. _____
3. _____
4. _____
5. _____
6. _____
7. _____
8. _____
9. _____
10. _____
11. _____
12._____
13. _____
14. _____
15. _____